When the Journey Seems Too Great

WHEN THE JOURNEY SEEMS TOO GREAT

CHARLES E. BLAIR

Tyndale House
Publishers, Inc.
Wheaton, Illinois

Unless otherwise noted, Scripture quotations are
from *The Holy Bible,* New International Version,
copyright 1978, 1984 by New York International
Bible Society.

First printing, October 1988

Library of Congress Catalog Card Number 88-72040
ISBN 0-8423-7997-5
Copyright 1988 by Charles E. Blair

CONTENTS

FOREWORD

I know Charles Blair, his wife, his children, and his
grandchildren. I've known him from a distance and from
close up. I've seen him riding high, basking in the glare
and glow of success, and I've seen him humiliated, wishing
he could hide in faraway anonymity. I've known the man
behind the abilities, the publicity, the true and false
accusations, the failures. I'm his friend.

Friendship, however, is not a static thing. It exists at
different levels and often fluctuates through time, distance,
and circumstances. Strong and stable friendships need
cultivation, attention.

Our friendship began many years ago with my
ministering to his church congregation and discovering a
personable man about my own age who had great dreams
of helping the aged in their years of inaction, suffering, and
infirmity. This high and commendable goal began to find
expression in bricks, mortar, buildings—a hospital. I
watched the developments with admiration and
thankfulness.

But when it looked like certain success, the vision

ultimately became a nightmare. During this period of dissolving dreams, our friendship dissolved too, and for years was nothing more than a memory. But God worked in mysterious ways.

Through a series of unplanned contacts, our paths crossed and crisscrossed again. Friendship entered a testing, questioning stage, which evolved into a different kind of relationship—more mature, trusting, reciprocal. I found a different man than I first knew. Perhaps we had both grown a bit through the years, but he had been on a long desert journey and had come through, though not without scars.

It was after this new birth of friendship that under God's clear direction I conceived the idea of the "Second Mile," project and volunteered to give it leadership. "Second Mile" was a move to help my friend recover financially.

It seemed that any association with Blair made me a co-conspirator in the problem, regardless of my motive or intention. The press did their proverbial hatchet job until I became almost as paranoid as Blair had been.

Charles Blair himself long ago had taken as his motto, "No attack, no defense." I've seen Blair deceived by his colleagues—yet never attack; manipulated by so-called friends—yet never lash out; falsely accused by the press—yet never vindicate himself; viciously maligned by angry enemies—yet never retaliate or descend into self-pity.

This is not to say he hasn't made serious mistakes and had his weaknesses exploited. This is no whitewash. But he has persevered, stayed at his post, and paid back more than 18 million dollars—an uncommon feat in anybody's book!

Though Betty Blair's name is not on the cover, she has been the steady soldier, notonly absorbing her own share of misjudgment and pain but encouragingly standing by her oftentimes bruised husband.

So my friend speaks not from hearsay. He's taken the

hard journey himself. He's been in the furnace. And the Fourth Man has stood beside him. What he says is worth hearing.

J. Allan Petersen

PREFACE

A decade ago, I began a journey through difficulties far beyond anything I could have imagined. I was then pastor of Calvary Temple, founder and president of both the Life Center and of the Charles E. Blair Foundation—all located in Denver, Colorado. In the process of selling bonds to underwrite these ministries, a serious breach of the law pertaining to investors and investments occurred. As founder-president and pastor, I could not help being the central target in the controversy and court proceedings that followed. Nor could I help condemning myself for the neglect, resulting from an overloaded schedule, which produced an incredibly painful harvest.

I was indicted by the grand jury and found myself in criminal court as a defendant. Then, to my inexpressible shock, I was declared guilty of fraud. The sense of humiliation that swept over me is beyond my words to express. My self-esteem floundered as did my Christian influence. A thousand or more people dropped away from our congreegation at Calvary Temple. I did not blame them for, to all appearances, I was rightly condemned and discredited.

I knew also that being involved in a church whose pastor had been convicted of a felony would be embarrassing.

I, Charles Blair, who had known a string of God-given successes for twenty-five years, experienced failure that, to my intense grief, was even more spectacular than the successes. In the midst of these circumstances I could easily have become a castaway, a dropout from the ministry, an embittered man with broken health. Thank God, because of his sustaining grace, these things did not happen. Today, I still pastor the same church, and as a congregation we are experiencing a deep move of God. The congregation is growing and moving forward. We stand in awe at the faithfulness of God.

I am enjoying good health. I did not have a nervous breakdown or develop stomach ulcers. Nor did I have to resort to tranquilizers (though I do not condemn anyone who does so under acute distress). That I came through these experiences as I did is a testimony that God can and will give us strength to cope with emotional stress—even that produced by twentieth-century pressures.

You know as well as I that the emotional stress brought on by a crisis situation is often harder to resolve than the problem itself. Long after the dust has settled and life has returned to a somewhat normal state, the self-recrimination, the pain suffered from loss of reputation and possessions, the haunting "might-have-beens," the unanswered challenges to our faith, remain.

Emotional stress can trigger wrong reactions and decisions if we do not keep our feet on solid ground. In my own turmoil I found myself searching for a good foothold, and found it in the truths I had lived by and had taught throughout my ministry. This time, those truths were tested in a greater way than I could ever have anticipated.

The firm ground I discovered was of four kinds—

persons, principles, promises, and prophecies.

Scripture shows that God usually chooses and works through persons. He created us in his own image, and he intends each of us to be a living, growing, vulnerable, real person. In the process of living—if we are not careful—we can become self-imagined personages. That is, we take on self-assumed images. Such an illusory mask may even seem to be thrust upon us. We come to see ourselves in a certain image and then strive to live accordingly. The energy it takes to do so causes great emotional stress.

Further, God intended that we should live by principles—his own eternal principles. For example, it is never right to do wrong, for right is never wrong and wrong is never right.

In addition, God makes certain promises on which we may base our faith. An example of such a promise is, "Call to me and I will answer you and tell you great and unsearchable things you do not know" (Jer. 33:3). Our faith is based not on wishful thinking but on fact—the promises of God to his people.

Those principles and promises are not just cold, hard facts—they are linked to a living, personal God. Our faith is not trust in a principle but in a person—God himself and his commitment to us.

Also, to those men and women who build their lives on those eternal principles and rest their faith on Scripture promises, God gives certain prophecies. He tells them what the end result of that kind of life will be. The Psalmist pictured it for us: "He [the upright man] is like a tree planted by streams of water, which yields its fruit in season and whose leaf does not wither. Whatever he does prospers" (Ps. 1:3).

As the pressures mounted, I went back again and again to the principles and the promises given in the Word. As painful and confusing emotions tore my mind and heart, God, in his mercy, helped me to understand that I dare not react on the basis of my "feelings." I came to realize anew some basic truths:

1. *Emotions come unbidden.* Emotions rush to the surface without our willing them to do so. In that sense, they are beyond our control. We can no more make ourselves feel loving than we can refuse to feel angry.

2. *We can—and we must—choose whether emotions will control us or we control them.*

3. *Emotions are a mixed lot.* We seldom experience only one emotion at a time.

4. *It is not sinful to have emotions.* They are a natural human response. Sin occurs only when we allow wrong reactions because of those emotions.

5. *The emotional response to a present situation is colored by and strongly linked to experiences of the past.* The unconscious is filled with memories. We may be able to block the details of an unpleasant experience from our conscious memory, but we do not have this same control over the hurts associated with that memory. When something happens in the *now,* it may trigger a response in the subconscious to a similar hurt in the past.

6. *Emotions that are buried alive will continue to eat at us.*

7. *Situations do not cause emotional stress unless there is conflict.* An incident becomes a problem when there is a conflict between what I think I should do and what I

want to do. That is described in Galatians 5:17 as the war between "the sinful nature and the Spirit." My human reaction may be to strike back, while the spiritual or godly response would be to turn the other cheek. My response may be to run away, to avoid the problem, while God may be directing me to stay and, with his help, to resolve it.

In this book I want to take you into God's Word and to share with you some of my own experiences that helped me to keep my sanity and spiritual equilibrium in the midst of great emotional stress.

I write not as a psychiatrist nor even as a theologian. I speak as a fellow human being, out of my own experience. I speak also as an observer of people. For more than forty years in the ministry I have been watching and listening day after day to men and women from various walks of life. Some of them have opened their hearts freely and shared their inner struggles. Others have made confessions. The behavior of still others has revealed that on the inside they were broken, shattered, and suffering.

This book is my simple witness to the fact that with God's help we can learn to cope with emotional stress.

CHAPTER ONE
INSIDE FAILURE

I want to open the door and take you into some of the darkest hours of my life.

The year was 1976; the place, Vail, Colorado. I had gone there for a prayer retreat following my criminal trial. Friends had loaned my wife, Betty, and me a condo and, in a real sense, I sought to hide from the world. I even grew a beard. I couldn't stand the sight of my own face.

I searched for a place to pray, away from the condo and the village. I found it in an aspen grove high on the mountainside. I went there at five o'clock each morning, wrapped myself in my sleeping bag to ward off the morning chill, watched the sun come up, and prayed.

Well, I tried to pray. Often I found myself reliving the events of the past weeks and months. The jury's verdict rang over and over in my mind as I felt again the devastation and despair of those moments. I felt as though everything I had lived for—my life, my ministry—had come to an end.

The jury had found me guilty of failing to assure that adequate information was given to certain investors (seventeen in all) who purchased securities that had helped to make the ministries of Calvary Temple, Life Center, and the Charles E. Blair Foundation possible. I knew that I was not guilty of intentionally or knowingly failing to give any information that should have been given to those who purchased securities. However, the jury felt that I, as president of the corporations, had the ultimate responsibility for making sure that all necessary information had been given by representatives of the corporations.

When the verdict was given on Friday, August 13, I was devastated. That evening and for days to come I was a zombie. I went through the motions of eating but I was unaware of the food on the plate. I got into bed but I couldn't sleep. I kept reliving that courtroom scene over and over again. I'm sure there were many phone calls. Either my wife or Gene Martin, a close friend who was staying in our home, answered them. The children and grandchildren were in and out—I don't know what I said to them. I was in a fog, detached from reality somehow.

I had promised my congregation I would be in church on Sunday, but I wondered after the guilty verdict if I could fulfill that promise. I wasn't sure my legs would carry me there. How could I face the people?

Again, I did not sleep Saturday night. Instead, I walked the floor or lay in bed wide-eyed, staring at the ceiling. I had promised the congregation I would be there because I had been sure the verdict would be "not guilty." But now I wondered whether or not I shouldn't simply send a message to be read.

No. I promised I would be there, and I had to go. Would the press be there? The angry investors? Would I be booed out of the pulpit? What would be the reaction of the congregation? I knew they must have been embarrassed by all the newspaper coverage of the trial and verdict. I wondered if this would be the inglorious ending of my ministry or if they would be supportive. Since their pastor had been convicted of a felony, would they stay around to help pay off the indebtedness or would they all scatter?

The unknown haunted me. I walked on rubber legs that Sunday morning, from the car to my study, and then to the pulpit. I was still in a state of shock.

Never again would I experience such an outpouring of love as I did that day! As I walked to the pulpit, the congregation rose to their feet in a standing ovation of loving support. A reporter wrote of that morning, "There was something genuine about the support that crowd gave. It wasn't anything staged. You couldn't buy it with money. It was genuine and it was real."

In a true sense, it was also life-giving. The energy of that crowd carried me through the morning. As soon as the benediction for the third service was given, I slipped away, leaving Gene Martin, who was also a minister, to shepherd the people for the next three weeks. I shall always be grateful to him for his leadership and caring during those very troubled days.

As for myself, I knew there was only One to whom I could go in that black moment—God the Father. I felt that the only way I could put my life back together was to get alone with him and once again hear his voice; that somehow through prayer I must find God's purpose for my life from that moment on.

So, I had gone to my mountain retreat, and the early mornings found me hidden away in my place of prayer. I determined to stay alone long enough and get quiet enough to reevaluate and to find God's answer to my question, "Where do I go from here?"

In those days, I felt a wide range of emotions—from moments of deep depression, fear, and tears to tremendous times of inspiration, when my spirit seemed to be caught away into God's presence. I spent a lot of time reading and meditating.

One morning as the first rays of light cut through the morning fog, my mind went back to another foggy day in 1947. The place was Edinburgh, Scotland.

Betty and I, as young evangelists, were there ministering when we received a cablegram inviting us to pastor a small, struggling church in Denver, Colorado. Our first reaction was to refuse. We were having a ball traveling the world. The thought of settling down to a pastorate just wasn't very appealing. It didn't take us long to come to a decision, and soon I was on the way to send a return cable, declining the invitation.

As I walked down Edinburgh's famous Princess Street to the cable office, I felt strangely impressed that I should wait and pray again. Somewhat perplexed, I turned around and returned to our hotel room.

Betty and I then made this a matter of daily prayer. Then, in an unusual way, the Lord spoke to us through the words of Revelation 3:8: "See, I have placed before you an open door that no one can shut." We both sensed that it was God telling us that we were to accept the invitation and go to Denver to pastor the church, which was then called Central Assembly, at the corner of Fourth Avenue and Grant Street.

Soon we found ourselves pastoring approximately seventy adult members and a hundred in Sunday school. At the end of that first year, the congregation was smaller still. We were young, and we were learning. I sought counsel from successful pastors on how to pastor a successful church and reach a city for God. Among those I visited were Dr. Robert Lee, pastor of Bellevue Baptist Church in Memphis, Tennessee; Dr. Louis Evans, pastor of Hollywood Presbyterian Church; and Henrietta Mears, director of Christian education at Hollywood Presbyterian Church. By 1952, our little church had grown to a thousand members and a building program was necessary. Many shook their heads in skepticism when they saw the scale of our vision.

The purchase of the property at Alameda and University and the building of the physical facilities were indeed tremendous projects. The task was not undertaken lightly. We had no money, nor did we have professional fund-raisers. Since we were not able to arrange conventional financing, we decided to borrow from our friends in the church and from the people of our great city and state through the sale of bonds.

We wanted to be as thoughtful of our investors as possible, so we told those who purchased bonds that if they needed their money before the due date they could redeem their bonds on demand. To my knowledge, we were able to keep that commitment.

Every phase of the construction was a challenge. We never had a surplus of funds and often we came down to the wire. We had no success formula. We simply walked softly before the Lord, step by step, with fear and trembling. At last, in June of 1955, we had the ribbon-cutting ceremonies, and our congregation moved into its present facilities.

As I continued in prayer there in the aspen grove one morning, I became aware that the sun now stood on the horizon, calling the mountain to life. Feeling the warmth of the sun and watching the sun climb, I thought again of Calvary Temple in the early seventies. It, too, was a rising sun attracting people from all over who came to Denver to see "how it was done."

I found myself in constant demand as a speaker for churches and leadership meetings. It seemed I could go nearly anywhere in the world I wanted to go, do just about anything I really wanted to do.

While all this was happening, a subtle change was occurring in my life. I began to be mechanical and to operate like a machine. My prayers were for more success. Often my missionary trips were to take photographs to show the people back home, to raise more money to go on another trip. It was really an ego trip! No, I didn't know it. The terrible thing about pride is, it is deceptive. "Pride goes before destruction, a haughty spirit before a fall" (Prov. 16:18).

The November 1974 issue of *Christian Life* magazine, in its survey of the one hundred largest Sunday schools in North America, listed Calvary Temple as seventh in size. That same survey listed our church as the fourth largest in gross income. Our total giving for the year of 1947 had been $14,000; in 1973 the total was $2,040,000.

At that time, we were in the largest expansion of our ministry. As the staff grew in size, the issues became more complex, the demands on my time increased, and I failed to continue to supervise as I ought to have. I learned to my sorrow that . . .

Unless you inspect, you sometimes do not get what you expect.

Calvary Temple had launched a new building program, which included a new sanctuary designed to seat 5,000. A model and the schematics had already been completed; the land had been purchased. In fact, more than eighteen years of effort had gone into securing some of the choicest property in southeast Denver. Just as we had done in the past, we were planning to build by raising funds through cash gifts and the sale of bonds.

The new sanctuary was only one of three major projects in which I was involved. In 1964, in response to a dream I felt God had given me to care for the sick of our city in a distinctive, evangelical atmosphere, the Life Center Corporation was formed. Our dream was to build a hospital to care for the whole man.

Life Center was patterned along the lines suggested by the Committee on Medicine and Religion of the American Medical Association, a facility designed to treat the whole man, physically, emotionally, spiritually, and socially.

Life Center was a nonprofit interdenominational medical complex, designed to serve people of all faiths. In addition to caring for intermediate and long-term patients, the projected facility would provide physical and occupational therapy to outpatients, speech and hearing therapy, individual and family psychological and psychiatric counseling as well as spiritual counseling by clergymen.

When an opportunity came in 1966 to purchase a large unfinished hospital, I felt this was an answer to my growing vision and burden. A place to treat the whole man— physically, spiritually, and mentally. Distinguished Christian leaders such as Dr. Vernon Grounds, Dr. Ted Engstrom, Dr. Armand Nicoli, and others became the first board members. Hundreds of wonderful investors also believed in the dream, and we all watched with gratitude as the building developed and the doors opened with 350 of the possible 500 beds available.

We called it *Life Center,* and that was so descriptive of what it was designed to be—a center of care, healing, rehabilitation, and life.

It seemed proper to underwrite the construction of Life Center just as we had done for projects at Calvary Temple. A Life Center Department of Development was organized and commissioned to carry out the selling of bonds. Again we borrowed from our friends in the church and outside the church. We promised these people that if they needed their money before the maturity date on their bonds that we would return it to them, just as we had done in the past.

While all this was happening, the Charles E. Blair Foundation, organized to expand our television and other media ministries, was busy developing a unique TV series, called *Better World.* This outreach was also partly underwritten by the sale of bonds. In 1974 the Foundation was just beginning to release the *Better World* series. We were on a hundred markets nationwide and the response was tremendous. But with the cost of air time we had only begun to recoup the upfront production costs on the films.

Ours was an image of success, but underneath the strain was beginning to show. The spiraling interest rates and increased building and operating costs were taking their toll. The financial stress was building, but with God's help we felt we were weathering the strain.

Even as I replayed these memories there in my prayer retreat on the mountainside, my reprieve was broken by a peal of thunder, drawing my attention to a distant mountain peak, where storm clouds were gathering. Often such mountain storms blew in quickly, with rain coming down even as the sun was still shining, so I pondered whether I should run for shelter. However, this' time the threat didn't appear imminent so I chose to stay there in the aspen grove. Even as I sat there, watching the distant downpour, another series of storm clouds filled my thoughts.

At Life Center, we never seriously believed certain things would happen, but they did. With all those projects going at the same time and costs escalating, we found ourselves in a severe financial bind. As we had done before, we prayed.

But this time nothing happened! The miracle that always
came to give us the last-minute reprieve did not come.
We tried everything we knew, but the day came when we
were unable to meet a scheduled payment to the investors.
The rest is history.

Whenever something like this occurs, the Securities and
Exchange Commission (SEC) becomes involved and an
investigation is launched. Immediately, the investigation
made it "news," and much of it was handled by the media
with something less than a sympathetic slant. While under
investigation, we were not permitted to sell or resell any
securities. With no cash reserve, we were unable to keep
our promise of redeeming bonds on demand. Also, fund-
raising became more and more difficult. As a result, our
financial position worsened and we were forced to file for
Chapter Eleven in bankruptcy court. Chapter Eleven
proceedings allow a corporation time to work out
a plan for repayment to its creditors, which is voted on by
the creditors, and then a time frame is established in which
payments will be made.

The findings of the SEC alleged that approximately
twenty of the total number of investors had not been given
the printed prospectus. Such an omission suggests fraud, so
the case was given to the grand jury. The charge was made
and verified by witnesses that some investors had not been
given the printed prospectus. When the vote was taken in
the grand jury, my indictment hung on one vote. After two
years of recurring delay, the criminal trial was held.

The arguments centered around whether or not I, as
president of the corporation, was aware of this oversight. I
was pictured as a leader who was tuned in to the smallest
of details, so the case was made that I must also have been
aware that a prospectus was not left with every investor.
Examples of my attention to detail included memos taken

from our files in which I drew attention to the misspelling of a word in a printed brochure.

It is true that I am a person who is concerned with details. Because of this, we had carefully prepared the printed prospectus, trained our salesmen, and set up a procedure to follow, which included leaving a prospectus with every investor. For some reason, this procedure was not followed in a few instances, according to the testimony in court. Seventeen people testified that they did not receive a prospectus from our salesmen.

We were unable to convince the jury that I had no knowledge of this discrepancy. The court held me, as the president of Life Center and the Foundation and pastor of Calvary Temple, responsible.

Before and during the criminal trial, I was in endless sessions with lawyers and courtroom appearances as the three corporations involved—Calvary Temple, Life Center, and the Foundation—filed for Chapter Eleven in bankruptcy court and gradually worked their way through the complicated procedures. We were in a difficult bind. It seemed as though our days were divided between courtroom appearances and raising funds to obtain release from the bankruptcy court with a plan for quarterly payments to investors of the three entities. This schedule put an incredible strain, not only on me, but also on our entire staff, and congregation as a whole.

From the beginning, we had had legal counsel for all three corporations. In fact, for several years we had in-house legal counsel at Life Center. Although the law was vague in regard to the procedure to be followed by nonprofit organizations in selling bonds, we sought to fulfill all the legal obligations.

As I had sat in criminal court and listened to the testimony against me, I hurt for those investors who testified and for other investors who sat with the spectators. Many were in financial need because of their investments.

I'm sure there were some who wanted me to be convicted. I looked into their eyes and my heart reached out to them because I knew they had been hurt. I was sure some of them, at least, thought I had gained personally, that by some manipulation I had taken what they had invested and used it selfishly.

I could not have faced them if I hadn't had a clear conscience. I never had any intention of deceiving anyone. At no time had I ever intended to hurt Christ or his Church or any of these people. I had not received a salary from Life Center or the Foundation, nor a commission of any size from the sale of any of the bonds. I had not misappropriated funds associated with Calvary Temple, Life Center, or the Foundation. Yet, on August 13, the headlines would read, "Pastor Blair Guilty of Fraud."

The stress of the criminal trial—traumatic as it had been—was exceeded by the inner struggle in the days that followed.

There, in my mountain prayer sanctuary, I started the long, slow process of putting my life back together. I knew the first step was to try to find God's purpose for my life from that point. I remembered reading a significant observation by Dr. Elton Trueblood: "Man cannot live well, either in poverty or abundance, unless he sees some real meaning and purpose in life."

Dr. William Sadler, a psychiatrist, echoed this truth: "Happiness is going somewhere wholeheartedly without regret or reservation."

Some years before this, in Riverside, California, I had shared the platform with Dr. Robert Steinberg, a Jewish psychologist and convert to Christianity. I remembered his saying:

One of the major problems I am facing today in my family counseling is that most Christian families have no clearly defined goals. They get up in the morning to go to work, to come home at the end of the day to go to bed, to get up in the morning to go to work, only to go home to go to bed . . . and so on. It isn't long before boredom sets in and life loses its luster.

It didn't take a lot of insight to realize that in the face of such devastating problems as I was then facing, it was of critical importance to have a sense of purpose. I felt I could never preach another sermon . . . that I couldn't remain as pastor in the same church I had pastored all those years.

There were those who agreed. Some ministers and lay people were saying I should quit the ministry, that I was a disgrace. They reminded me how God's Word teaches that a leader must be above reproach in his conduct, inside and outside the church.

I couldn't deny the "truth" in their statements. Indeed, I had preached from those same texts. As I struggled with their accusations and my own temptation to quit and get away from the mess, I had to ask the question, "If a man of God fails, does that mean that God is through with him, that he no longer has any future?" At the same time I could not get away from the inner realization that, although my wish was to leave the ministry, God had not released me from my calling.

So I sought counsel. One godly colleague to whom I went listened patiently and then suggested, "Charles, the answer is in the Word. Open your Bible and start reading in Genesis and read until you find a man with a similar kind of problem. Study his life carefully and see how God dealt with him."

I did that, morning after morning, there in that grove of

trees on the mountainside. I searched in the Scriptures for the man through whose life God would speak to me. I felt drawn to Moses. I read that he felt he was such a failure and so inadequate for the task that when God called him to deliver the Israelites, he responded, "O, Lord, please send somebody else to do it."

There is nothing more devastating than to be called upon to do something and to feel that you are not adequate to do it because you have failed in the past.

I wanted nothing more than to do as Moses had done—to run away, to build a new life. I had neither the inclination nor the desire to face the task that was ahead. I wasn't sure how far the love of the congregation would stretch nor if the demand to repay the investors could, in fact, be met. In Calvary Temple alone, we were committed to a five-year repayment plan—five years of large quarterly payments. In addition to the financial stress, there was a congregation of hurting people who needed ministry and a battle-weary staff to consider. In addition, I faced the task of raising funds to meet quarterly payments to the Life Center and Foundation creditors. The task overwhelmed me. I thought I knew how Moses felt.

Although Moses was an Israelite, he had been adopted by Pharaoh's daughter; therefore, he was brought up and educated in Pharaoh's palace. As a young man, however, he identified with his own people and apparently envisioned himself as their deliverer. In any event, he got ahead of God.

How familiar it all sounded! Moses saw an Israelite slave quarreling with an Egyptian overseer. Moses came to the aid of the Israelite and, in the scuffle, he killed the Egyptian and buried him in the sand. Later the news reached

Pharaoh, so Moses, in fear of his life, fled to the backside of the desert.

From his own point of view, and that of others as well, Moses had failed. Despite prospects of a great future, he did what a lot of people do when they fail—he ran away. Changing his life-style, he went from being a prince in a palace to a shepherd on the backside of the desert. Moses tried to put his calling behind him, to forget his dream. But God did not forget Moses.

This story of Moses was very reassuring, as I realized that God had not recoiled from Moses when he had failed so miserably. God was as much with Moses in the desert as he had been with him in the palace. It is easy for us to think of God in human terms. Because those we love sometimes desert us when we fail, we suppose that God also distances himself from us when we fail. I have learned that the opposite is true.

Forty years after he ran away, eighty-year-old Moses was watching the sheep of his father-in-law. His attention was suddenly drawn to a bush that was burning. Because of intense desert heat, and occasional flashes of lightning, dry bushes sometimes catch fire and are quickly consumed. Moses noticed that although this bush was burning, it was not being consumed. Curious, he turned aside to look. God spoke out of the bush and said, "Moses."

There in my lonely mountain retreat, I began to sense anew that God still knew my name and he knew where I was. Not just my location—he knew exactly where I was in my pain and confusion.

Moses' response to God was, "Here I am."

Then came the voice again, "I am the God of your fathers—Abraham, Isaac and Jacob." That passage ends with this significant sentence: "At this, Moses hid his face because he was afraid to look at God." Moses was ashamed to look at God because he saw himself as a failure.

Moses then asked God three questions, and in those questions and God's answers I began to find the way out of my devastation.

Moses' first question to God was, "Who am I, that I should go to Pharaoh and bring the Israelites out of Egypt?" From his point of view, he was a wanted man, a fugitive from Pharaoh. Moses was really saying, "God, I tried once— don't you remember? I failed. I blew it. Who am I that you would choose me to do this?"

I like God's answer. He simply replied, "I will be with you."

In essence, I heard God saying to Moses—and to me, "I took a wad of nothing, threw it into nowhere, and it became the earth you stand upon. I can take you, Moses, and I can use you because I am going to be with you."

God wasn't depending only on Moses to get the job done. God wanted to work *through* him. Slowly, I became aware that God didn't need my supposed cleverness; I didn't need to have all the answers. My most important requirement would be to lean on him for wisdom and help.

It was an awesome moment when I realized that God still wanted to use me. I realized that God looks for a person who will be a channel of blessing in his name; also that I had not become unusable to God because I had failed.

I began my ascent out of failure when I began to change my thinking. Just as Moses wondered if the people would still want him as a leader, I wondered if my congregation would still want me. In light of my failure, with the subsequent disgrace and reproach I had brought on the church by having a part in plunging them into debt, I wondered if they would ever be able to tolerate me as a leader. In the midst of my confusion and pain, I came to realize that God could still use me and if I would learn to lean on him and be a channel, he would work through me and bless other lives.

Moses raised a second question, which was quite understandable. He asked, "Suppose I go to the Israelites and say to them, "The God of your fathers has sent me to you" and they ask me, "What is his name?" Then what shall I tell them?"

Perhaps Moses was still remembering what one of the Israelites had said to him that day forty years before, when he had seen Moses kill the Egyptian. Moses had thought his act would be appreciated. He learned otherwise. The next day he found two Israelites quarreling. When he sought to intervene, one of them said, "Who made you a prince and ruler over us?" Moses had interpreted the message as meaning that the Israelites didn't want him as their leader.

Again, God gave Moses a beautiful answer: "You are to say to the Israelites, 'I AM has sent me to you' "

In other words, Moses was to be their leader by God's choice. As I pondered this, God gave me the inner assurance that he still had his hand on my life.

Failure accused me; failure told me I had no right to be used again by God.

In the midst of my failure God was saying to me, "I can use even your failure. Just as Satan tried to use your failure to destroy you, I will use your failure to transform you if you will learn to depend on me."

In seeking answers to the question—how could God use my failure?—I reviewed some of the basics of the Scriptures. I reminded myself that God has only good will toward his children. His will is to save and sustain us. Jesus said, "The thief comes only to steal and kill and destroy; I have come that they may have life, and have it to the full" (John 10:10).

In contrast, Satan wants only to distort and destroy, using two common strategies. First, he seeks to make us feel guilty and ashamed, to cause us to live in a state of doubt, to have all kinds of complexes and conflicts. By that ruse he tries to make us ineffective.

If he can't defeat us that way, Satan tries to make us feel self-sufficient and independent, to make us think we can make it on our own.

I reaffirmed the truth that I was not created to operate independently. I was designed to function best when I am dependent upon God.

I know God does not put a premium upon failure. The fact is, however, most of us do fail—some worse than others. God had not caused me to fall into failure. He did not wish evil upon me. On the other hand, the Word says that "God works for the good of those who love him" (Rom. 8:28). I know that somehow God can take even the shattered pieces of a life and create beauty. I was reminded of the artist who takes pieces of glass and creates a beautiful stained glass window. God could also take the broken pieces of my life—even my failure—and put the pieces together in a beautiful workmanship that would bring glory to his name.

Moses' third question was, "What if they do not believe me or listen to me and say, The Lord did not appear to you?"

Then God asked Moses, "What is that in your hand?" It was a shepherd's staff, a rod. At God's direction it became a staff of transformation. At Moses' word it would turn into a serpent, then back into a rod again. It was this staff Moses would stretch over the waters of the Nile and they would become blood. Later he would stretch the same staff over the waters of the Red Sea and they would part.

God was saying to Moses that he would provide the power, but he would use something that Moses had in his hand. No special equipment was needed.

Like Moses, I too had to come to realize that whether God could use me or not did not depend upon either my abilities or lack of them, either upon my successes or on my failures my clever plans or my lack of them. I saw that if God were to use me, it would be because of my dependence on him and my cooperation with him. Paul wrote, "Being confident of this, that he who began a good work in you will carry it on to completion until the day of Christ Jesus" (Phil. 1:6).

It was a great moment for me when I moved from self-sufficiency to God-sufficiency. That changeover took place when I realized that Moses became usable when he stopped focusing his attention upon his faults and weaknesses and began to draw upon God's abilities and God's sufficiency.

In the midst of failure, I learned that to fail does not make one a failure.

God was saying to me, "In the midst of this situation, don't focus your attention upon your failure."

I remember keenly a long interview Betty and I had in London, England, with the late Arnold Toynbee, the renowned historian. In reviewing past nations and civilizations, Mr. Toynbee remarked that when nations are challenged by catastrophes, how the nation responds to the challenge is most important. He mentioned how important it is that challenge be balanced with purpose.

I remembered those words and applied them to my life. I faced a challenge unlike any I had faced before. The question, of course, was what would my response be? Would I seek to find rest in flight, or would I stay and face the issues at hand.

Many times during our crisis I was asked, "Do you think you were acting in the will of God when you started Life Center?" I asked myself the same question many times, too.

I struggled with the answer until, finally, I realized that I was asking the wrong question. While in the midst of difficulty was not the time to probe and analyze the decisions and actions that got me there in the first place. The real issue was, "What was I going to do about it?"

My response to failure was more important than the failure itself.

I came away from my three-week prayer retreat with a fresh resolve and a knowledge that God was at work in my life. I had established three steps that I would take over and over again in the trying months and years to follow. These three steps I would recommend to anyone as a way out of failure:

1. *Find the will of God for today and do it.* Doing so will give a sense of purpose. Without a sense of purpose, death sets in, bringing with it periods of depression, frustration, and anxiety. In contrast, when a person matches his daily life with a mission, he comes alive. It is easy to get bogged down trying to anticipate the end results. Problems must be attacked one day at a time.

Moses was called the meekest man on earth, which simply means that even though he was a strong, dynamic leader—one of the greatest—he was humble. He was at peace within himself. He had found God's will and he was doing it.

As it was for Moses, the key to success is knowing what God wants us to do daily and doing that, one step at a time.

As God leads us and as we walk in obedience day after day, we find our way out of our problems.

2. *Change from emphasis on self to emphasis on God.* Mind power is limited. Will power is limited. Soul power is limited. However, when we as limited persons link our insufficiency and inabilities with the ability and the all-sufficiency of God, we become no-limit persons. It is not what we can do but what God can do through us that is decisive. Therefore, the important questions become, "Who is our Source? On whom are we leaning?"

3. *Discover God's how and when.* When Moses tried the first time, his timing was off. He operated on the assumption "I am the man of the hour." His idea was right but his method was wrong. Killing off the Egyptians one by one just didn't happen to be God's plan. Moses was correct as to the *what,* but he was wrong as to the *when* and the *how.* When he found God's timing and method, when he recognized that God was the source and that he was to be only the channel, Moses was able to accomplish his goals.

Perhaps the most important lesson I learned from my failure was this:

Don't write the ending to your life prematurely.

I came back to the city in the same fear and trembling that Moses experienced, to begin a long journey toward victory. As I look back to that experience, I believe it would have been a tragic mistake if I had allowed that failure to terminate my ministry. By studying the life of Moses, I found principles that became the solid ground I needed for the difficult months and years that were to follow.

The story of the last decade is a book in itself and much of it can be found in *The Man Who Could Do No Wrong*, which I wrote with the help of John and Elizabeth Sherrill (Chosen Books, 1981). To tell it as briefly as possible, each of the quarterly payments to the Calvary Temple investors was a miracle story. Finally the last payment was made in the fall of 1983.

An agreement was reached with the Life Center investors that allowed the hospital to be sold. It is now being run by another professional organization.

Today, I have a growing appreciation for the mercies of God, which are new every morning. I am more aware than ever before that walking in God's will must also be renewed in our hearts every morning or, at the very least, at every important decision point. I am constantly aware that knowing the *what* of God's will can be dangerous unless I wait for the *when* (God's timing) and the *how* (God's method).

STRESS STABILIZERS

The way out of failure is twofold:

1. Change your way of thinking. Know that:
   a. God can still use you. Failure does not make you unacceptable to God.
   b. God can use even your failure to bring glory to his Name.
2. In the midst of failure, don't act until you know:
   a. what God wants you to do,
   b. when he wants you to do it, and
   c. how he wants you to proceed.

C H A P T E R   T W O

THE SCARS REMAIN BUT THE POISON IS GONE

I have learned that forgiveness and forgetting do not happen simultaneously. Nor does forgetting follow automatically on the heels of forgiveness. Forgiveness is not spiritual amnesia, to borrow a phrase coined by David Augsburger. It is not blotting out all memory from our minds. Forgiving, or the healing of the memories, is a process of taking the poison out of the wounded spirit.

Life has a way of producing wounded spirits. Plans go wrong, misunderstandings arise, or we are treated unfairly. We sin and we are sinned against. It is easy for resulting wounds to become infected with resentment and bitterness. We want to be loving and forgiving, but some wounds go very deep, and "turning the other cheek," choosing to forgive, is not so simple. If we are not careful, what begins as resentment turns into bitterness.

Bitterness is not an emotion that comes and goes. It takes root and grows until eventually it encompasses one's spirit. That is why we are warned in the Word to be careful lest bitterness take root in our lives (Heb. 12:15).

Bitterness is the outrage of a wounded spirit. It can be enormously destructive.

In my own experiences of deep hurt, I discovered that getting rid of bitterness is not a one-time thing. I found that I had to keep applying forgiveness, time after time, every time the painful memories came back. I continued doing so until the poison was gone. On a daily basis, I had to deal with the deep hurt over the loss of the church's property.

When we went into the financial crisis in 1974, Calvary Temple owned prime property to the north and south of the present facilities. On one lot we had planned to build a new sanctuary. The architectural drawings had already been completed. I cannot adequately tell you how painful it was for me to see that dream melt into thin air.

It was determined that all the property—beyond the original sixteen acres owned by the church—had to be sold in order to speed up the repayment of investors. Because of the real estate market at the time, the church lost a great deal. Most important, we lost an opportunity that could never be recaptured.

With deep concern I wanted the investors to be repaid as quickly as possible. I understood the necessity of selling the property, but emotionally I had to deal with the inward hurt caused by the shattering of a dream—my dream of a project very dear to my heart.

I was constantly reminded of that frustration. I could not approach the church without driving by one tract or the other. Every time I saw one of them I hurt. As I watched a new subdivision being developed on those tracts of land, I would mentally envision the new sanctuary we had intended to build there, and my heart would ache. I felt that eighteen years of careful planning and working had gone down the drain.

I would either drive in or out of the church parking lot at least twice a day, and some days a half dozen or more times, and could not escape passing by one or the other. On a daily basis I had to deal with the hurt that seemed at times almost unbearable as the poison of those emotions rushed to the surface. Sometimes I would experience this pain as I was arriving to preach and would have to struggle to keep the anointing as I went to the pulpit. Or perhaps it would be at the end of a long day when I was emotionally and physically drained from being all day in committee meetings. Then I would toss and turn through the night. Those were traumatic times for me, days of emotional distress.

I went through stages of bitterness. I even thought I hated God at times. I "got mad" at people. I "got mad" at myself. Forgiving became a problem. Underneath it all, I knew I had to come to grips with those wrong reactions or leave town.

The process took months. Some days were worse than others. I had to forgive myself. I had to "forgive" God! I had to forgive others. Sometimes the emotions would surge rebelliously as I drove by the property. I would see the earth-moving equipment putting in the streets and getting ready to put in a new subdivision, and I would become almost physically ill. In my mind's eye I kept seeing what might have been: the beautiful sanctuary being built. And the battle would rage on.

Eventually, thanks to God, the wonderful day came when I could drive by and feel no hurt, when I could say, "Thank you, Lord, for the lessons learned from that experience."

I don't suppose the past and its consequences are ever completely forgotten. But I can say, from personal experience, that the time can come when the scars remain but the poison is gone! Of course, that kind of healing doesn't happen without our involvement. God has provided a way for the healing to take place, but we have to be involved in the process. We have to keep applying forgiveness until the healing comes.

The good news is that while we may never eradicate the past as far as memory is concerned, the sting and the poison can be eradicated. There can be healing for the deep wounds of the spirit.

The wounding of the spirit is just as real as a wound to the physical body. Though the spirit's wounds are a little harder to see, I think the pain is felt just as deeply, if not more so. As in the case of a physical wound, something must be done if healing is to occur in the wounded spirit. When we break a leg we go to the doctor and he sets the broken bone and puts on a cast. The cast does not heal the leg. It is an aid to the healing, but only the healing process within our bodies can cause the bones to knit together. In the same way, when we, in obedience, apply forgiveness, God will cause the wounded spirit to heal.

Our reaction to hurt usually follows a pattern. First, we discover that a person has betrayed our trust, and we feel the sting of hurt. Or, someone injures us in some way and we feel attacked. We may exclaim, "How could he (or she) do that to me?" We resent being treated in such a way.

Second, if we make the mistake of brooding over the hurt, bitterness sets in, and we find ourselves declaring, "He can't do that to me and get away with it. I'll show him!"

Finally, as bitterness grows, we devise a way to get even. We plot our revenge. This may be something we do to the person or it may be that we simply withdraw our friendship and love.

We have many ways to get even with people. Sometimes we break relationships with them. Or we run away and hide or do something to help us forget. Some of us change our life-styles. A few become ill and suffer nervous breakdowns so that we can justify our inability to cope with the situation. More often, we build walls around ourselves and go into emotional isolation.

None of these solutions brings peace but rather more pain. When we are hurt and we are struggling with the emotions of bitterness, we have three choices. It is not true that "we can't help it" or that we have no options. We make choices in our reactions to hurt. We make a choice whether we are conscious of doing so or not.

INTERNALIZE RESENTMENT

One choice we can make is to *internalize our feelings*, to bury our feelings of bitterness inside us. If we are strong disciplinarians and are able to keep a throttle on our feelings and keep them under control, we may be able to succeed at burying our resentments. However, kept inside and allowed to ferment, resentment becomes bitterness. The energy of bitterness is a strong force, which finds a way of seeping out into the body or mind. It may show up as nervousness, tension, stomach ulcers, migraine headaches, or half a dozen other miseries.

We don't fully realize the impact our emotions have on our physical bodies. William James, the renowned psychologist, many years ago said research had shown that the entire circulatory system forms a sort of sounding board in which every change of our consciousness, however slight, may make reverberations.

Hardly a sensation comes to us without sending waves of alternate constriction and dilation down the arteries of our arms. The blood vessels of the abdomen act reciprocally with those of the more outward parts. The bladder and bowels, the glands of the mouth, the throat, the skin, and the liver

*are known to be affected gravely in certain severe emotions
and are unquestionably affected transiently when the
emotions are of a lighter sort. That heartbeats and the
rhythm of breathing play a leading part in all emotions
whatsoever is a matter too notorious for proof. . . . Our
whole cubic capacity is sensibly alive; and each morsel of it
contributes its pulsations of feeling, dim or sharp, pleasant,
painful, or dubious, to that sense of personality that every
one of us unfailingly carries with him.*[1]

Submerged bitterness produces misery. Unpleasant
memories stored away, not in peace but in turmoil, will
come back to us in some kind of torment. It may be in the
form of fear, obsession, depression, neurosis, or psychosis.
If we don't bury a memory in peace, it will someday—in
some way—force itself to the surface.

In that sense, bitterness is similar to a timed-release
capsule. A certain cold medicine claims to give twelve hours
of relief. In each capsule are hundreds of different colored
grains of medicine. Once the capsule is swallowed, each
different color of grain dissolves within the body at a
different rate of speed. As a result, the medication keeps
working, hour after hour, for twelve hours.

In somewhat the same way, when we swallow the
capsule of bitterness and refuse to forgive, at unpredictable
intervals little droplets of poison are released to circulate in
our minds, bodies, and spirits. Bitterness acts like the
timed-release capsule except that it has no time limit. It
goes on and on poisoning us, until we determine to get it
out of our system.

Even from the medical and the psychological viewpoint,
anyone can see why it is not a good idea to internalize bitterness. Some claim that people who nurse an unforgiving
spirit probably will die prematurely. Most of us who have

battled with bitterness would certainly agree that it takes a physical toll on us. More important than the physical damage, nursing bitterness weakens our relationship with God.

An unforgiving spirit freezes our sensibilities, our reasoning faculties, even our responses.

When we allow ourselves to be ruled by bitterness, our emotions go numb as though they were paralyzed. We begin to suffer an inner bondage. We become uptight. The more bitterness we harbor, the greater the uptight feeling becomes, and the more numb our emotions and responses become.

A little boy was sent to the closet by his mother for being naughty. When the closet door was closed, he had a tantrum. He kicked his feet on the floor and pounded on the door. When he finally became silent, his mother decided to go look. She opened the door and there he sat. Angry, he looked up at her, his eyes red. In a rush of words, he said, "I spit on your dress; I spit on your shoes; I spit on your hat. And I'm sitting here waiting for more spit!"

I do not here suggest that a closet confinement is a good way to discipline children. But the boy's behavior illustrates what happens when we harbor bitterness and refuse to forgive. Unforgivingness freezes our spirit, our emotions, our responses. A frozen spirit loses its freedom to enjoy life fully.

When we harbor bitterness, we also develop a strange emotional tie, a form of enslavement, to the person we have not forgiven. Everything he or she does has a negative reaction on us. And the enslavement of unforgivingness ties us forever to our pain.

Harboring bitterness also limits our capacity to love.

Emotionally fragmented, a part of us is involved in estab-
lishing and maintaining loving relationships, while another
part is devoted to getting even, to destroying relationships.
The more we retain bitterness for more and more people,
the less energy is left for developing loving relationships.

EXTERNALIZE BITTERNESS

Internalizing resentments is clearly not the answer. A
second choice available to us in dealing with deep hurt is
to externalize our feelings by venting ourselves, allowing
the angry feelings and words to explode on those around
us. Expressing anger without some control is ineffective for
several reasons.

Innocent people may get hurt. If we take a shotgun and
shoot away at the landscape, we will hit something. If you
fling out words of anger and bitterness indiscriminately,
some innocent person standing nearby is bound to be
struck.

Whoever said, "Sticks and stones may break my bones,
but words will never hurt me" didn't know what he was
talking about. Words hurt, and they hurt deeply.

Norman Cousins, editor of *Saturday Review* for more
than a quarter century, is now on the faculty of the School
of Medicine at the University of California in Los Angeles.
His special field of study has been the biochemistry of the
emotions. He is especially interested in the way attitudes
and emotions can bring on disease or improve the
prospects of recovery. He said regarding the importance of
words:

*Words are weapons or building blocks. . . . Words, when
used by a doctor, can be gate-openers or gate-slammers.
They can open the way to recovery, or they can make a
patient dependent, tremulous, fearful, resistant. The right*

words can potentiate a patient, mobilize the will to live, and provide a congenial environment for heroic response. The wrong words can complicate the healing environment, which is no less central in the care of patients than the factual knowledge that goes into the physician's treatment.[2]

Indeed, words are powerful tools. They can also absolutely destroy deep love. When we speak in the heat of anger, we may say things we don't really mean and live to regret a thousand times.

Bitterness is contagious--another reason we should not externalize feelings haphazardly. Children catch bitter feelings from parents. Parents catch them from children, employers from employees, and vice versa. People who say, "From now on, I'm going to let my feelings all hang out; I'm going to give vent to them," will discover that such a response is not the answer. This doesn't mean that we are to ignore our anger or fail to recognize it. But, free expression of it without control or limitation does much more harm than good.

All of us will face problems that could make us bitter, if we allow them. But when we do become bitter, we then become responsible for causing others' hurt, whether we mean to or not. Our own hurt feelings cannot simply be pushed aside. It doesn't help us to say that it doesn't matter when it does. The fact that we are caring people—which is what we want to be—means that we are vulnerable to being hurt. When we attempt to shrug it off, we simply submerge those feelings and the hurt resurfaces as other symptoms, which explains why the doctor may ask you, "Who or what is eating you?"

Expressing our hurts, responding in angry words, may take care of our immediate feelings but it will not take care of our bitterness entirely.

NEUTRALIZE BITTERNESS BY FORGIVENESS

When bitter feelings threaten, a third option, one I highly recommend, is also available. We can choose to neutralize bitterness by forgiving the ones who have hurt us.

This was the option I chose. It wasn't easy, for it meant that I could not give in to feelings of self-pity. It meant working at the business of forgiving. I soon discovered, however, that the benefits were worth the effort.

Not everyone makes this choice. Not long ago, a Colorado judge was indicted by a grand jury. He was later cleared of all charges by the high court. In fact, in handing down the decision, the high court said that the case should never have been brought to trial. Somebody asked the judge if he was going back to the bench. He answered, "Yes, but I am bitter. I am bitter toward the press because they wrote articles that were untrue, biased, prejudiced, and full of half-truths. Furthermore, I have learned that the grand jury system is a farce because anybody can go to the grand jury and lead them, push them, influence them, and intimidate them. I am bitter. I have extremely high costs in attorney fees to prove my innocence. I am bitter."

I do not condemn the judge for his pain, but I do regret the way he apparently chose to deal with that bitterness. I do not believe that anyone in this world ought to be able to rob us of the joy of living in peace with God or with men.

A lady once came into my office for counseling. As we talked, a deep hatred surfaced for someone, whom she finally confessed was her mother-in-law. After we had talked for some time, I told her she had to get rid of her bitterness if she was ever to experience peace again.

As we talked I noticed she appeared to have arthritis. I'm not a doctor, but I did see that her knuckles were swollen and her fingers were cupped in. When she reached for a

Kleenex in her purse, I noticed that she had difficulty moving her fingers.

I talked to her about choosing to forgive her mother-in-law and asking for God's help in learning to love her. Then I led her in a prayer and asked her to repeat a prayer after me. When I got to the part of the prayer where I said, "God, I forgive my mother-in-law," she was unable to continue. Three times she broke down and couldn't speak her mother-in-law's name in prayer. The fourth time she got through it.

When I said good-bye to her, I asked her to repeat that prayer on the way home and to add, "I love you, _____." On her way home, a town about sixty miles north of Denver, she stopped at a pay phone and called me.

She reported, "As I've been driving along, I've been doing what you told me to do. I not only thanked God aloud that he was helping me to forgive my mother-in-law, but I have been asking that God would bless her. I prayed that I would truly love her. Do you know what happened, Pastor? The stiffness in my fingers is all gone! I can move them without effort! I'm having a 'camp meeting' right here in this telephone booth!"

I cannot guarantee you that if you love and forgive your enemies, whatever is wrong in your body will go away. I can't guarantee healing, but I can guarantee you a release in your spirit. When you love and forgive your enemies and the bitterness leaves your spirit, you will come alive and good things will begin to happen. It is amazing.

A judgment day is coming, a day of reckoning, when God will judge those who have caused others to suffer. But I, the sufferer, dare not allow bitterness to seethe within me, for if I do, I will be the loser. I must accept the antidote, the cure, which God gives. I must come to the place where I can commit the individual, the situation, the misrepresentation, into God's hands. I must able to say, "God, because you forgive me, I forgive them. Thank you for forgiving me. Cleanse me now from all bitterness."

Forgiveness is required also because unforgiveness hinders our prayers. Jesus said:

I tell you the truth, if anyone says to this mountain, "Go, throw yourself into the sea," and does not doubt in his heart but believes that what he says will happen, it will be done for him. Therefore I tell you, whatever you ask for in prayer, believe that you have received it, and it will be yours. (Mark 11:23-24)

Our Lord was giving to the disciples an eternal and absolute truth: If you believe and doubt not you will receive. There is great power and victory wrapped up in faith unmingled with doubt. But the promise is conditional. The very next verse says, "And when you stand praying, if you hold anything against anyone, forgive him, so that your Father in heaven may forgive you your sins" (v. 25; see also Matt. 6:12, 14-15).

The verse begins with the conjunction, "and," linking the phrases. In other words, maintaining a spirit of forgiveness is essential to our prayers being answered. When we refuse to forgive, we find ourselves unable to accept God's forgiveness. Emphasizing the tremendous impact of bitterness held within, Jesus told us to pray: "Forgive us our debts, as we also have forgiven our debtors." Jesus added, "If you forgive men when they sin against you, your heavenly Father will also forgive you. But if you do not forgive men their sins, your Father will not forgive your sins" (Matt. 6:14).

Admittedly, our Lord's answer to bitterness goes against ordinary human nature. To choose to forgive does not satisfy our natural desire for revenge. This choice is possible only for the Christian who depends on the energy of the indwelling Holy Spirit. Note our Lord's words, "Love your enemies, do good to those who hate you, bless those who curse you, pray for those who mistreat you" (Luke 6:27).

How can we really forgive someone who injures us? Jesus gives us in this verse four keys: (1) love, (2) bless, (3) do good, and (4) pray. Those are the responses of the Spirit-controlled person.

KEYS TO FORGIVING ANOTHER
Key #1: Love. The love we speak of here is *agape* love. It is love that acts. It reaches out. This kind of love launches a campaign, a strategy, a bombardment. *Agape* love is not merely an emotional feeling; it is something we do. The word *love* appears 150 times in the New Testament and means "a divine drive toward unity of that which is separated." It is love that comes from God, which enters our hearts by the Holy Spirit (Rom. 5:5), and flows through us to the person in need of that love and forgiveness.

To love is to accept the person as he is, a human being just like you and me. To love is to seek to understand the *why* behind the deed or word. To love is to ask oneself, "Am I misinterpreting what happened? Or am I over-reacting? What part, if any, did I play in this misunderstanding?"

I discovered that one reason I had a problem in loving was because I had never learned to receive love. Evidently, in my childhood something developed in my inner being that made it difficult for me to accept love. My great joy was to love others and to see that others were taken care of—which eventually led me, perhaps, to the ministry. It was never easy, however, for me to accept love from others.

I tended to discount their words and acts, since I didn't see myself as lovable.

As I reflected on the genuine love and forgiveness that was so generously being offered to me, I began to say, "Lord, perhaps one of my really serious problems is that I haven't reached out to take the love being given to me."

It wasn't easy. Often, even as I tried, I found myself slipping back into the old patterns. But as I allowed myself to receive love, I found it even easier to reach out in love to those around me. I began to understand that love is a circle. As we learn to know God and love God with all our hearts and reach out in love to our neighbors, and allow those around us to express their love back to us, the circle becomes complete.

Key #2: Bless. To bless is to affirm the individual's worth before God. To bless is to wish divine blessing and prosperity for the individual. When we first do this and the hurt is still with us, we may have to do it as an act of faith. We have to act lovingly before we begin to feel loving. We must act in obedience to the Word, leaving our feelings for God to change. We can choose to act according to our feelings or in spite of them.

To bless is also to give up our desire for revenge or to get even. God's Word says, "Do not take revenge, my friends, but leave room for God's wrath, for it is written: 'It is mine to avenge; I will repay,' says the Lord" (Rom. 12:19). God reserves vengeance for himself. Why? Because only God is capable of seeing the situation clearly from all sides. He, the source of justice, is the only worthy judge.

Key #3: Do good. Now this is hard—really hard. It certainly goes against the grain, especially when we are hurting. But it is effective. Nothing can restore a broken relationship as quickly as doing a kind deed, because an act of goodness can free us from bitterness. It is difficult to grasp our bitterness tightly when we are reaching out in love to touch someone.

Key #4: Pray. I have discovered experientially that I can't hate someone and at the same time pray sincerely for him. When I began to pray for my enemies, I discovered that I stepped over to their side of the situation. I stood on their side, so to speak, and asked God to move in their behalf. It was amazing what happened. Sometimes, I received new insight into the situation. But always, as I continued to pray, God gave me love. Then the feelings of anger or bitterness began to go.

Telling the Lord all about the situation also demands my own honesty. For example, when I share a hurt with a friend, I tend to put myself in the best light possible, which is only human. Most of us tend to color the story in subtle ways, but it is hard to do this when we are kneeling before God. He sees behind our words and into our motives—and we know he sees more clearly than we do.

We have to deal with the chip that may be on our shoulder. We are not able to see ourselves as God sees us or as others see us. Before we react in ways that which we may later be ashamed of, we need to get alone with God. "Be still, and know that I am God" (Ps. 46:10). We need to ask and receive forgiveness for any wrong on our part.

DEALING WITH THE FEELINGS OF HURT
Ridding ourselves of bitterness is a spiritual battle, especially if the bitter feelings have taken root. They don't leave easily. It *feels* so good to nurse our hurts! Sometimes the feelings are so deep that we are overwhelmed, and we wonder if it is possible ever to love that person again. The only effective

place to start winning the battle over feelings is on our knees.

When I find myself harboring bitterness, I have learned to take time to review the entire matter with the Lord. I recognize that I need to be honest and express my feelings. I also know I cannot shock God. He already knows exactly what is in my heart. I admit that these feelings have a hold on me and that I am helpless to get rid of them. Then I visualize taking all those feelings of hurt, anger, and bitterness in my hands and holding them out to the Lord. In faith, I ask God to empty my hands, to take away those feelings and, in their place, to fill me with his love, as he has promised: "God has poured his love into our hearts" (Rom. 5:5). We cannot reach out to help someone else until our own pain is healed. Jesus said that he came to heal the brokenhearted (Luke 4:18). We must accept the promise of his gift of inner healing. We must also ask him to do what we ourselves cannot do by all the salve of self-pity that we might apply. We must ask God to heal our wounded spirit.

When the old feelings threaten to return, we can refuse, by an act of the will, to accept them. By faith we can say, "I have given these feelings over to God. From this moment on I will consider only thoughts of goodwill toward this person."

STRESS STABILIZERS
Forgiveness is not spiritual amnesia:
1. Deciding to forgive doesn't blot out all memory of the past. The healing of a wounded spirit is a process—it takes time.
2. You may never eradicate the past as far as memory is concerned, but the sting and the poison can be extracted.

3. Healing can come for the deep wounds of the spirit. The scars may remain, but the poison will be gone.

NOTES

1. Magda B. Arnold, ed., *The Nature of Emotions* (New York: Penguin Books, 1968), 21-22.
2. Norman Cousins, *The Healing Heart* (New York: Avon Books, 1984), 112, 131.

CHAPTER THREE
WHY ME, GOD?

Suddenly—without warning—I began to be nauseated. My
friend Dr. Jerry Falwell and I were having breakfast in the
Holiday Inn coffee shop in downtown Denver. We were
undergoing similar kinds of problems. He, too, had run into
difficulty in the sale of securities in expanding his ministries
in Lynchburg, Virginia. He was there in Denver, having held
a fund-raising rally with his supporters the night before. In
his case, there had been no grand jury indictment or other
charges filed. He had simply been advised to surround
himself with qualified men and raise the funds to repay the
investors. When he came to see me, he was doing exactly
that.

The more Jerry talked, the sicker I became. Both of us
had raised funds in much the same way with the same
purpose: to extend God's kingdom. I found myself
questioning how two ministries could be
involved in similar situations and the outcome be so
different. One leader was indicted and one was not. As I
mentally reviewed my situation, I knew that in all three
corporations we had been very careful to have a

prospectus prepared. We had also worked to operate within all legal restrictions. Yet, seventeen people testified that a salesman failed to leave a prospectus with them. And, as a result, I was indicted by the grand jury. Even as Dr. Falwell and I talked, I faced trial on those charges.

As we sat there at the breakfast table, Jerry and I talked of a mutual friend, Rex Humbard, and similar financial difficulties he was facing at that time. Mentally comparing my situation with these two friends, I felt I had been treated unfairly. Suddenly a great swell of emotion was pushing its way to the surface. Unaware of my dilemma, Jerry went on talking. He had come to spend this time with me to encourage me. We were both in the depths of the heartache of our experiences.

Part of what Jerry and I were going through was the result of a series of investigations begun in the early seventies into the procedures of nonprofit organizations that were selling securities. The laws concerning nonprofit organizations were not always clear to those issuing such bonds. Organizations selling these securities were trying to interpret the law correctly as it related to them. As a result, some had a printed prospectus listing their assets, liabilities, and general financial state, while others did not.

Naturally, when word gets out that an organization is being investigated, it casts a cloud of suspicion over it, making fund-raising even more difficult. Because of high interest rates, the state of the economy, and the fact that many nonprofit organizations operated on a limited cash flow, others like ours soon found themselves in financial trouble.

As I sat there talking with Jerry, the full impact of the situation hit me. Neither he nor others had been indicted or found guilty of fraud. Perhaps we had, in our organization, made careless or innocent mistakes.

Somehow they had been able to avoid them. For some reason God in his sovereign grace had allowed my own situation to go differently. I had no ill will toward either of them. It never crossed my mind to wish my experience on them. But an overwhelming surge of resentment and anger toward God was making me ill.

I found myself crying out, "God, why me?"

To my great relief we were soon interrupted by Jerry's pilot who came to tell him it was time to leave for the airport. Reaching for my last bit of control, I managed to say a warm good-bye, and then head for the parking garage—my dignity intact.

I headed my car down three levels of a curving, cement exit. Feeling very woozy, I alternated between driving too fast and slamming on my brakes. I wanted to get out of there as fast as possible. As soon as I was outside, I rolled down the window to let in the cold air and started toward the church. I got as far as Cheesman Park, in central Denver, stopped the car, turned the motor off, opened the door, and vomited.

There in the park I cried out to God. Reacting out of self-pity and deep resentment, full of confusion and frustration, I was angry. It appeared that God was playing favorites, even though I knew that the Scriptures teach otherwise. At that moment my emotions were overriding my reason. Rather than placing my faith in God and his Word, I was allowing myself to be swept along by powerful emotions. All I could see was that I was indicted and facing a criminal trial, even though I felt I was innocent. In my heart of hearts, I knew that my only motive had been to help people. My resentment came from feeling that I was not such a bad a person, that my character was not so full of impurities and flaws as to deserve such treatment from God.

My image of God was of one who could do anything and that nothing was too hard for him. He owned the cattle on a thousand hills—his resources were unlimited.

I made the mistake of assuming that because God could not fail, neither could I.

I had begun to think it would be dishonoring to God for me to fail, that no matter how far I stepped out in faith, God would run in at the last moment to shore up my projects and keep me from failing. The time had come when God chose not to do so, and I was shattered.

I saw clearly, as I was sitting there in the car that I had come to a turning point in my ministry and my relationship with God. Even as I struggled with my anger, I became aware that I was in a spiritual battle. Something had come within me that was not of God; something I can only describe as a mental poison.

I drove back to the church, parked the car, hurried in, and made a beeline for the altar. I didn't stop to talk to anyone. I was desperate. I knew I dared not surrender to this emotion and allow the seeming inequity of the situation to overwhelm me.

I fell at the altar and literally bellowed out to God for help. As I wept, the realization began to come that there are some circumstances in life that can never fully be understood by us in this life on earth. In the light of that, I began to see that my responsibility was to serve God, to move in submissiveness, to say, "Not my will but yours be done." In that hour, also, I learned another truth:

I need God more than he needs me.

God has a way of raising some people up and setting

others aside. I acknowledged in that hour that God could have set me aside. The world would have gone on without me. I would have become simply another statistic, another ministerial fatality, another man of God gone wrong.

I had come face to face with God's sovereignty. And God spoke to me, deep in my inner spirit, saying, "Charles, remember, I told you at the very onset that Satan would try to wreck your ministry, your spiritual life, and your health—physical and mental. But if you will turn to me, I will see you through. I will pour strength into your inner being."

I prayed, "God, I don't see how you can get any glory out of this, but since I have to come down either on the side of belief or unbelief, I choose to take my stand on your eternal Word. Since I am limited in my understanding and faith, I lay on this altar my own inability to judge and weigh this situation. I place all in your hands. I submit to your plan for me."

I stayed at the altar until I felt inner peace again. Yet, even as I walked down the hall to my office, I realized that I had as yet won only "round one" in the contest.

As I struggled to deal with the question of God's sovereignty, I went back to the Word again and again. And I discovered, as I had before, that my experience was not new. I was not alone. In dealing with my own anger at God and my reluctance to accept his sovereignty, my attention was drawn to Jonah. He, too, was a man angry at God. In fact, he mounted a one-man protest against him. He had been called of God to preach in Nineveh, but, as you know, he disobeyed and boarded a ship sailing in the opposite direction. The next scene was a strange storm, and Jonah was thrown overboard and swallowed by a huge fish. In that abnormal extremity he repented and in the end was vomited up on the seashore. Then he went to Nineveh and delivered the message God had given him.

God has unusual ways of dealing with people. "Truth stranger than fiction" grossly understates the story of God's dealing with Jonah.

One day when I was getting a haircut, a stranger walked into the barbershop and sat in the chair next to mine. He didn't know me, nor I him. He began to make fun of the Bible and the stories in it. It was an interesting moment! The barbershop became strangely quiet because most of the men there knew that I was a pastor in the city. The man, not knowing this, continued to wax eloquent. After he had finished making light of the story of a whale swallowing a man, my barber said very quietly to me, "Pastor, do you believe the stories in the Bible?"

I try not to let an opportunity pass to share my faith, especially when there is a captive audience, so I said, "Yes, I do. I believe every line in the Bible and I will tell you why. God is so much a God of detail . . ." I went on to talk about the tides going out and coming in and how they can be predicted to the very split second. I told about the bobolinks coming out of Canada, going down in early spring to South Carolina, and in June to Cuba; in August they go to the Andes in Brazil. Then the next spring they fly back to the very same trees in Canada from whence they came.

Then I said, "I believe God can do anything. He can create a fish big enough to swallow a man and have that fish at the precise spot where he needs him. Yes, I believe every word of the Bible. If the Bible had said that God had put running water and electricity in that whale's belly I would have believed that too." By the time I finished, it was very quiet in that barbershop!

Truth much stranger than fiction! Jonah told his story:

*The word of the Lord came to Jonah. . . . "Go to the great
city of Nineveh and preach against it, because its
wickedness has come up before me." But Jonah ran away
from the Lord and headed for Tarshish. He went down to
Joppa, where he found a ship bound for that port. . . . He
went aboard and sailed for Tarshish to flee from the Lord.
(Jonah 1:1-3)*

Reading between the lines, I can see the prophet,
stalking around—angry at what God had told him to do.
Since he felt Nineveh deserved to be destroyed, he was in
no mood to go preach to them, knowing there was always
the possibility that they would repent and God would
change his mind. Jonah, deciding to run away, found a
vessel leaving for the west, paid his fare, and went aboard.

A price had to be paid, whether Jonah went east or west.
For us also, whether we go God's direction or not, a price
has to be paid.

Jonah got aboard the ship all right, but God intervened
in a most unusual way.

*The Lord sent a great wind on the sea, and such a violent
storm arose that the ship threatened to break up. . . . Then
the sailors said to each other, "Come, let us cast lots to find
out who is responsible for this calamity" . . . and the lot fell
on Jonah. . . . The sea was getting rougher and rougher. So
they asked him, "What should we do to you to make the sea
calm down for us?" "Pick me up and throw me into the
sea," he replied. . . . Then they took Jonah and threw him
overboard, and the raging sea grew calm. . . . But the Lord
provided a great fish to swallow Jonah, and Jonah was
inside the fish three days and three nights. (Jonah 1:4-17)*

I can picture Jonah, angrily protesting against Almighty

God. He had been trying to put enough space between himself and God so that God wouldn't see him. Sooner or later each of us must learn the lesson that we cannot hide from God. David had learned this lesson, as shown in his prayer:

Where can I go from your Spirit? Where can I flee from your presence? If I go up to the heavens, you are there; if I make my bed in the depths, you are there. If I rise on the wings of the dawn, if I settle on the far side of the sea, even here your hand will guide me, your right hand will hold me fast. If I say, "Surely the darkness will hide me and the light become night around me," even the darkness will not be dark to you; the night will shine like the day, for darkness is as light to you. (Psalm 139:7-12)

God will follow us down the longest road, into the darkest night. He has a thousand ways to reach us, to talk to us, to persuade us to obey him and to go his way instead of our own. When God sent the storm, the sailors began to throw the cargo overboard in order to lighten the load, to keep the ship from breaking apart. It didn't work, for the sea became rougher and rougher. They cried to their heathen gods, but no answer came. As was their custom, they cast lots to determine who might be causing the anger of the gods. Casting lots was a means used frequently in ancient times to settle disputes. It was an appeal to the gods (by the heathen) and to God (by the Hebrews) to procure a just settlement in a dispute.

When the lot fell on Jonah, he confessed that his disobedience was the cause of the storm. Not every storm comes from God, nor does every storm come because we have been disobedient. But the story of Jonah indicates that some calamities do occur because of a person's disobedience. Jonah knew that this storm was because of him.

Jonah admitted his guilt. He suggested, "Why don't you just pick me up and throw me into the sea?" Now that was easy enough to say, not so easy to make happen. Finally, after they had tried everything else, they complied, and the sea became calm.

We know, too, deep within us, when the storms we experience are direct results of our disobedience. Though we cause some of our own storms, others come not of our own doing. In any case, storms are never an end in themselves. We should never think that God allows a storm just because he likes to upset our little boat. God not only sent Jonah a storm, he sent a means of rescue, and the way he did it is remarkable. As far as we know, he had never done it before, nor has he since. And I doubt if he will ever do it again. God, in a unique way, provided a tailor-made rescue. He matched the storm and the rescue to the person and the situation.

Most of us have experienced the sinking feeling of going down in a really fast express elevator or of being on a passenger jet when it hits an air pocket. Some of us can remember what the downward swoops of a roller coaster do to our stomachs. A few years ago I went on one with my grandson and thought I would die before the end of the run.

I have tried to imagine the sinking feeling that Jonah must have had, feeling himself go deeper and deeper into the waters.

But the Lord provided. Just as the Lord had sent the great wind on the sea, he also provided a great fish to swallow Jonah. Jonah was inside that fish for three days and three nights. I've tried to imagine the feeling of being swallowed, and what it would feel like with the undulant motions of the fish through the deep waters hour after hour. Three days he had to "sweat it out." Of all the strange classrooms of discipline—the belly of a whale!

It is no surprise to learn that Jonah prayed. And God intervened, which is no surprise either, because the God who sends the storm, and then sends the means of rescue, is ready to hear prayer, even from such a strange prayer room as the belly of a whale.

Jonah's prayer, as recorded in the Bible was:

From the depths of the grave I called. . . . I have been banished from your sight. . . . The engulfing waters threatened me. . . . Seaweed was wrapped around my head. . . . When my life was ebbing away, I remembered you, Lord. . . . But I, with a song of thanksgiving, will sacrifice to you. What I have vowed I will make good. Salvation comes from the Lord. (Jonah 2:2-10)

In today's language, my guess is that it would have sounded more like:

I'm just about done for. If this is hell, I want out! . . . I can't stand the feeling of separation, of not feeling the comfort of your presence . . . . Help, Lord, I'm drowning. . . . This slimy seaweed keeps slapping me in the face! . . . I'm going down for the third time. . . . There's no other God I want to serve. Only you can save me. I'll go to Nineveh! I'll go, God, I'll go!

And the Scriptures say, "And the Lord commanded the fish, and it vomited Jonah onto dry land" (2:10).

I think Jonah was ready for something dry, and ready to go to Nineveh—ready to go east. God does not make us do anything. He has given us a will of our own. However, he can make us willing to do his will.

You can lead a horse to water, but you can't make him drink, we often hear. But you can put salt in the oats and make him thirsty, making him much more willing to drink. God has a way of putting salt in our "oats." He has a way of making us willing to do his will.

Jonah went to Nineveh and preached as God had commanded him.

Jonah obeyed the word of the Lord and went to Nineveh. . . . He proclaimed: "Forty more days and Nineveh will be overturned." . . . They declared a fast, and all of them, from the greatest to the least, put on sackcloth. When news reached the king of Nineveh . . . he issued a proclamation . . . "Let everyone call urgently on God. Let them give up their evil ways and their violence. Who knows? God may yet relent and with compassion turn from his fierce anger so that we will not perish." (Jonah 3:3-9)

What a development! As a result of Jonah's sermon, a proclamation from the king, and the repentance of the people, God had great compassion and intervened in the city of Nineveh. "When God saw what they did and how they turned from their evil ways, he had compassion and did not bring upon them the destruction he had threatened" (3:10).

Whenever you and I repent, God intervenes. But when Jonah saw this, he got angry, upset with God because he did not destroy Nineveh.

But Jonah was greatly displeased and became angry. He prayed to the Lord, "O Lord, is this not what I said when I was still at home? That is why I was so quick to flee to Tarshish. I knew that you are a gracious and compassionate God, slow to anger and abounding in love, a God who relents from sending calamity. Now, O Lord, take away my life, for it is better for me to die than to live." (Jonah 4:1-3)

Why in the world would Jonah get angry because God sent a spiritual awakening to Nineveh? To understand, you need to know the historical significance of Nineveh and Jonah's beliefs regarding Israel. Jonah believed that only Israel deserved the blessing of God. He believed that God blessed Israel in two ways, first through special spiritual and temporal gifts and, second, by sending calamities on all Israel's enemies.

Assyria was the rising world empire, destined to destroy Israel. Nineveh was its capital city. The notorious brutality of the Assyrians was such as to make the surrounding peoples shudder with terror. The Assyrians were the Nazis of their day. Because the Assyrians had been unusually cruel to the Israelites, Jonah thought the Ninevites deserved punishment. When the almost unbelievable announcement came from God that Nineveh was to be destroyed within forty days, the heart of Jonah must have leaped with a sudden sense of relief. Besides being a prophet he was a man of Israel and an ardent patriot. The Great Judge had passed sentence—if Nineveh perished, then Israel's position was definitely more secure. No doubt, Jonah feared that if Nineveh turned and repented God would relent, Assyria would be spared, and Israel would be jeopardized.

When God had compassion and spared the enemies of the Israelites, Jonah could not understand. How could God show compassion upon the wicked, ruthless enemies of Israel? The "goings on of God" were mysterious to him and he rebelled.

When we get confused, it is easy to be led into frustration and despair. When we get into despair, we may say

with the prophet: "O God, I would rather die than live."
Strange, God doesn't let us die in those times because the
storm has come to teach us a lesson. God has a plan, a
lesson that we must learn. God taught Jonah a lesson,
which I believe he wants also to teach us today:

God uses people we wouldn't choose.
He answers prayers in ways we don't understand.

Isaiah wrote, "His understanding no one can fathom"
(40:28), and " 'My thoughts are not your thoughts, neither
are your ways my ways,' declares the Lord" (55:8). Paul
wrote, "How unsearchable his judgments, and his paths
beyond tracing out!" (Rom. 11:33).

God's ways are not our ways. His thoughts are not our
thoughts. God wants to teach us that he uses people
different from those we would select. He goes about the
answer much differently from the way we would. God says
to us: "I want you to let me run the affairs of this world
and trust me that what I do will be for your good."

God's first response to Jonah was to ask him a question.
Notice that God did not reject Jonah because he got angry,
but he did address Jonah's anger. He asked, "Have you any
right to be angry?" In other words, "Have I acted against
my nature? Have I been untrue to my word?"

Jonah didn't reply. Instead he went east of the city, built
himself a temporary shelter, and sat down to see what God
would do. He acted as though his anger would change
God's mind, as though God would demonstrate his love for
Israel by raining down judgment on a city of repenting
people.

God then gave to Jonah a beautiful object lesson of how
much he loved and valued people. God provided a vine
that grew up around the shelter, increasing the shade, and

easing Jonah's physical discomfort. Then God sent a worm that chewed away at the vine and caused it to die. Then a scorching east wind came, drying up the vine, and making Jonah even more miserable. When Jonah expressed his anger over the death of the vine, God compared his sense of injustice at the destruction of the vine to his total lack of feeling for a city of 800,000 people.

Anger can warp our perspective and cause us to accuse God of wrongdoing.

The late Bob Pierce, founder of World Vision, preached one of his last sermons at Calvary Temple. Bob was afflicted with leukemia, from which he died. He was too weak to stand, so he sat in an easy chair on our platform telling us his story. I have edited a portion from his message that evening. I was deeply moved as I heard this dear man of God talk of his struggle with God's sovereignty. This is part of the story Bob told:

At the end of my life I have had one daughter take her life by suicide. This daughter was the closest to me . . . he was the most like me. She had given her heart to Jesus when she was five years old. Time and time again she flew to the mission field to minister with me. While I was flat on my back in a hospital in Switzerland, burned out from typhoid I had contracted in Vietnam . . . away from everybody because I couldn't cope with any stress . . . my doctor called me one day and said, "Your daughter has just taken her life."

Just a few days later I received a letter that Sharon had written two weeks before in which she was screaming for help. I'll never know why that letter took two weeks to get to me. It should have taken only three or four days. I

*anguished, if only I had gotten the letter on time, I would
have known. . . . I felt I could have saved her.*

   *Don't think I didn't have bitterness in my heart.
I tell you, I shook my fist at heaven. I had preached the
gospel for forty years when that happened . . . thirty-five of
them all over the world.*

   *I had said, "Lord, if you'll take care of my three children,
I promise I'll devote my life to caring for the orphans and
widows. I'll make the sacrifice of absence from home and
from my wife, I'll take on the responsibility of being an
offering-taker, a money-raiser for missions."*

   *When my daughter took her life, I said, "God, you broke
your promise. I did my part but you did not do yours."*

   *I didn't know how to fit this into anything I knew about
the promises of God in Scripture or anything else. I felt God
had failed me. I went through the roughest time of my life.*

   *I lay in that hospital bed for several weeks and fussed
with God and thrashed, but God didn't hit me with a bolt of
lightning. He could have. The first time I shook my fist at
him, he could have wiped me out, but he didn't—because
he loves me. When I gave myself away to him forever, he
took me. God takes care of what he prizes.*

   *But God is reckless with what he does to make the most of
what he prizes. He is not delicate. One of the most valuable
things that you can experience is to come to know that no
matter how God is dealing with you and no matter how
rough it goes, it's his love that's doing it. In the end—I don't
care whether you agree to anything or not or get anything
resolved or not—in the end, God still loves you.*

   *As I come to the end of my life, I have come to know that
God is absolutely true. . . . You can spend your life drawing
incomparable comfort from every promise in the Scripture,
but you will constantly have to be prepared for the jolt that
comes to try your faith to the utmost. Life doesn't happen the*

way you preconceive it will happen. Deliverance may not be what you preconceive it to be. The provision for the supplying of your needs may not be what you thought it would. Being tested to the limit of what you are able to bear may not be what you prepackaged it or perceived it to be.

The measure of your faith and devotion and conse-cration to Jesus Christ comes right down to the one word— faith. *Faith is the God-given inner resource that helps you to endure that which happens—even if you can't accept it—to face life and acknowledge it and take it as it is . . . and still know that God is God and he still loves you.*

It took faith for me to believe that God loved me amid all that had happened; but that has always been the price of growth. God's children learn the most by their failures and by their adversities. You have to know that faith is daring to step out into the dark and take the consequences. Faith is stepping off a cliff into the dark and believing that the hand of God will be there to catch you. If the hand of God hap-pens to have a lot of rocks in it when you land, you just have to have faith and say that it is God and it is going to work out all right; and it does. That's what I wanted to tell you: it does! At the end of my road it does, it does, it does, it does.

Jesus is who he says he is . . . and what he says he will do he does. But there isn't any way I can package it into a neat little formula and hand it to you so that it explains everything in advance.

As Bob spoke that night, I realized anew that life is so designed that sooner or later each of us has to deal with the weighty problem of God's sovereignty. The moment comes when we are face to face with the claims of Christ, with the fact that following Christ means recognizing God's sovereignty in our lives and the lives of our loved ones.

We must come to the realization that if we are truly his, we are no longer in control—God is!

The Apostle Paul wrote, "You were bought at a price. Therefore honor God with your body" (1 Cor. 6:20).

If such an experience has not happened to you, it will. The time comes when each of us asks, "Why me, God?" The 'whys' may surface out of deep hurt and confusion. A situation may arise when we, in agony of spirit, find ourselves grappling with resentment toward God the Father.

In that hour, I believe God would come to each of us through his Word as he came to Jonah and to Bob Pierce. In our uncertainty, God tells us, "Don't carry the weight of uncertainty. Trust me as your God to work it out." "And we know that in all things God works for the good of those who love him" (Rom. 8:28).

STRESS STABILIZERS
1. God does not desert us in our anger. His love is greater than our anger.
2. God uses people we wouldn't choose. He answers prayers in ways we often don't understand.
3. God's sovereignty means he has the right to decide the direction our lives will take. When we truly submit our lives into his hands, then the "Why me?" question ceases, and peace comes.

CHAPTER FOUR
GRAPPLING WITH DEPRESSION

A few years ago, on November 15, Victoria Pellegrino jumped seventeen stories to her death. Friends felt that she had everything—she was attractive, dynamic, and a successful author. Five years before her death,. she coauthored a best-seller, *The Book of Hope—How Women Can Overcome Depression*, following her own personal struggle with depression.

In her *Book of Hope,* she wrote that suicide is a result of a person having no available options, that "suicide grows out of a profound sense of hopelessness." In the closing pages she made the statement: "You have to keep trying to find your lost self through your own efforts, your own strength. These are the wellsprings of your own hopefulness."

At the time of her death, Vickie was completing her fourth book, entitled *The Other Side of Thirty*. Friends who talked to Vickie on the last day of her life said that she talked in "monotones and that she sounded lower in spirit than they had ever heard her before." It seems the wellsprings of her own hopefulness had gone dry.

In the words of one observer, "There seemed to be no other way, so she took her own life."

I think I can understand Vickie's death because I too know a little bit about depression and the power it can hold over a person. When you get so low you have to look up to see bottom, you know you are depressed. When the image that you've had of yourself—a man whom the people of a city have treated royally for twenty-five years and given almost every honor that a citizen could want to have—is swept away and you find yourself in disgrace, it is depressing!

I remember the day when the grand jury issued an indictment, stating that I would have to stand trial. I volunteered to go to jail the next morning. If a person doesn't go, they come after him. I had been to jail dozens of times to visit prisoners and to preach. I never dreamed I would ever have to go to be fingerprinted. This was to be the first of many humiliating experiences.

When I walked in, I was met by a big Indian, about six feet tall. He told me, "Twenty years ago I was riding to work in my car, listening to a radio broadcast called Prayertime. That day the preacher said, 'I am going to pray a penitent prayer and I want everybody listening to me who has never accepted Jesus Christ before to pray with me.' I prayed that prayer, and I became a Christian twenty years ago. Little did I dream that one day I would take the fingerprints of the preacher who had led me to Christ."

I could have fallen through the floor. I was embarrassed. I was humiliated. There really wasn't much I could say.

I wiped the ink off my fingers and went across the hall to the "mug room" to have my picture taken. When we walked in—there was another gentleman with me—the man sitting there asked, "Which one is Blair?" I sheepishly raised my hand and he said, "Wait till I tell my wife. She watches you on television every Sunday."

Those experiences were just a drop in the bucket when compared with the embarrassment I had to suffer in the months and years that followed. There seemed to be no end to it. It felt like a black cloud hanging over me, or a weight upon my shoulders. For a time I grappled with depression almost daily.

I know how the woman felt who came to me after I preached one Sunday and said, "Pastor, I heard you say a few weeks ago, 'When you get to the end of the rope, tie a knot and hang on.' What I need to know today is when you have done all that, how do you keep hanging on?" A lot of people are asking the same question.

I have learned from personal experience that depression causes us to be troubled and perplexed, to have an ache inside that cuts deep into our inner being. When I am depressed I have difficulty in controlling my feelings. Depression warps my thinking and isolates me from those who love me. When I become depressed I begin to think wrongly. For example, I would be hurting and at the same time trying to cover up my pain. At the same time I wanted those closest to me—my spouse, my children, my staff—to recognize how much I was hurting and to come to my aid.

Depression causes us to isolate ourselves.

Of course, I didn't tell anyone I was hurting—I just supposed they would know. My attitude was that if they were really paying attention, they would see my pain. I expected them to be mind readers! All the while I struggled to put on a front, and I was disappointed when I was successful! At times I was so convincing that no one guessed how I was hurting. It was cruel pride that kept me from reaching out to those who could have helped me just by being with me.

From my experience of working with others, I think the covering up of pain is a common problem. We get depressed, we cover our feelings, and when others—our spouse, our friends, our employer, the preacher—don't read our minds and try to come to our rescue, we become angry and shut them out. Our pain drives us deeper and deeper into depression.

In the end, by our silence and our self-defensiveness, we isolate ourselves from the very people we need most. We retreat into our hurt and build the wall still higher as our depression deepens.

A very dear man in our congregation fell into this trap. He got into deep financial problems, was without a job, and really needed his pastor to pray and believe God with him. He and his wife have been faithful to the church, having served on nearly every committee. They were the kind of people I could always count on when I needed help. If I asked, they were there ready to give of themselves to the church. Now they were in need, and I didn't know what was happening.

He decided to stay home from church to get my attention. I did miss them, even though our church is quite large. I usually miss the faithful members when they are not in their usual pews on Sunday. I assumed he was away on business or on vacation. There was a nagging question, but no one had mentioned that family to me, so I kept expecting them to turn up and tell me about their vacation trip or wherever they had been. When that didn't happen, I called him. His response was to tell me how hurt he had been at my apparent lack of concern.

He is a precious brother, and we were able to talk through the hurt. In the course of the time together, I confronted him with what I stated earlier. You and I have a responsibility when we are in need to share our pain—to speak up to those who care about us. When we retreat silently into our hurt, we make it nearly impossible for others to minister to us.

Depression has been called the social disease of our times and, from my own experience in working with people, I think it may well be true. Two studies were done recently. In 1977 the Commission on Mental Health gave its annual report to the president and to the general public. The report stated that at any one time 25 percent of our population is under such emotional stress to be considered as suffering from depression or anxiety. The report also said that 15 percent of that group are of school age, and a large percentage of this group, to my surprise, are over 65.

One of the most comprehensive surveys ever undertaken of mental health in America is now underway. The initial results indicate that at any given time 29 million Americans—nearly one in five adults—suffer from some kind of psychiatric disorder, mild to serious. This survey, being conducted by the National Institute of Mental Health, will ultimately involve interviews with 20,000 people, door-to-door, in three major cities. This is five times as many people as have been involved in previous health studies.

Christianity Today, in reporting on recent studies, estimated that "up to 10 percent of the U.S. population may be experiencing a significant level of depression. A substantial portion of that group is seriously depressed and despairing of life itself."[1]

Depression shadows the steps of the godly.

Depression affects all age groups, from the very young to the very old. It even takes hold of many of God's people.

And we are shocked. We hear so much about abundant living and joy being the heritage of the Christian that we don't know how to respond when a leader we admire succumbs to depression. Or, we find ourselves overwhelmed by problems. Depression surrounds us, and suddenly we panic. We act as though some strange thing has come upon us and tell ourselves that if we were really full of faith, and if we had what it takes spiritually, such disturbances wouldn't happen.

We compound the problem by berating ourselves. Part of the solution in dealing with depression lies in recognizing that it is a common human problem. Depression shadows the steps of the godly as well as the ungodly. In my own times of deep depression, I found guidance from God in studying the life of Elijah. The Book of James reminds us that Elijah was an ordinary man, yet he was mightily used of God in a dramatic confrontation with King Ahab at a time when the nation of Israel was deep in idolatry. Even the fearless and fiery Elijah had to battle depression.

Elijah lived in unusual times. After King Solomon's death, civil war had erupted, and the nation of Israel had been divided into the northern kingdom called Israel and the southern kingdom called Judah. Jeroboam ruled Israel, and Rehoboam, Judah.

In order to break the natural ties of his people to Jerusalem, the capital of Judah, King Jeroboam established two other centers of worship in Israel, one in Bethel, the other in Dan, acts forbidden by God in the Scriptures. Jeroboam also appointed his own priests and established his own religious festivals. He then fashioned two golden calves, which some believe were imitations of the two exquisite golden cherubim of Solomon's temple and supposedly designed them to represent the God of Israel.

He placed one south in a temple at Bethel and the other north in Dan.

Each of the kings who succeeded Jeroboam followed in his footsteps, each becoming progressively more sinful. It was said of Omri, father of King Ahab, that he did worse than all those who were before him (1 Kings 16:25). It was he who arranged the marriage of Ahab to Jezebel, the daughter of an idolatrous Phoenician family. Her family worshiped Baal, the god of a lascivious religion, which included both female and male prostitution in its worship.

Jezebel had determined to remove completely all worship of Jehovah and to replace it with the worship of Baal. Under her influence, the temple in Samaria was rededicated to the worship of Baal, followed by persecution of the worshipers of Jehovah and the killing of many faithful prophets. Only those who were hidden away in caves survived the slaughter.

King Ahab, the seventh in a line of ungodly kings, reigned at the time Elijah was called of God to minister. That idolatrous regime created a situation in which any dissenter's life was in jeopardy. Courageous Elijah's first move was to confront King Ahab face to face. In obedience to God, Elijah made this declaration: "As the Lord, the God of Israel, lives, whom I serve, there will be neither dew nor rain in the next few years except at my word" (1 Kings 17:1).

That declaration did not make Elijah popular, especially when, just as he had predicted, a famine came. As the intensity of the famine increased, so did Ahab's search for the prophet. Elijah had a price on his head. In the third year of famine, Elijah again suddenly confronted King Ahab. This time he challenged the king to the famous prayer duel on Mount Carmel between the prophets of Baal and himself, a prophet of Jehovah. On that fateful day, Elijah's opponents numbered 450. While the people of Israel looked on, Elijah challenged the them:

How long will you waver between two opinions? If the Lord is God, follow him; but if Baal is God, follow him. . . . I am the only one of the Lord's prophets left, but Baal has four hundred and fifty prophets. Get two bulls for us. Let them choose one for themselves, and let them cut it into pieces and put it on the wood but not set fire to it. I will prepare the other bull and put it on the wood but not set fire to it. Then you call on the name of your god, and I will call on the name of the Lord. The god who answers by fire—he is God. (1 Kings 18:21-24)

All day the prophets of Baal prayed, becoming more and more frantic as the evening drew near. "But there was no response; no one answered" (1 Kings 18:29).

When they gave up, even as the sun was setting, Elijah ordered that twelve earthen pots of water be poured over his sacrifice. Then he prayed, and fire fell from heaven. It consumed the sacrifice, the wood, the stones, and even licked up the water around the altar.

When the people saw it, "they fell prostrate and cried, 'The Lord—he is God! The Lord—he is God!' " (1 Kings 18:39). Then Elijah led the children of Israel in a mass execution of the 450 false prophets.

The power of God was still so strong upon Elijah that, after all of this, he ran in front of Ahab's chariot all the way into the city of Jezreel—a distance of eighteen to twenty miles.

Obviously, not everyone was happy with Elijah's triumph—especially Jezebel. She sent Elijah the message: "May the gods deal with me, be it ever so severely, if by this time tomorrow I do not make your life like that of one of them" (1 Kings 19:2).

Hearing this, Elijah ran for his life. He traveled first with his servant. Then he left him and went alone a day's journey into the wilderness. Finally, exhausted, emotionally drained, and thoroughly depressed, he dropped under a broom tree. Before he fell into an exhausted sleep he said, "I have had enough, Lord. . . . Take my life; I am no better than my ancestors" (1 Kings 19:4).

After he had slept for some time, Elijah was awakened by an angel who told him, "Get up and eat." He looked around and saw bread and water. After he had eaten, Elijah went to sleep again.

A second time the angel came, woke Elijah, and said, "Get up and eat, for the journey is too much for you."

That could be said of many of us today: the journey of life has simply become too much. Our lives seem to be out of control. We find ourselves slipping into hopelessness and depression. There seem to be no available options.

I think I know how Elijah felt. There were many times during the past decade when I didn't think I could take one more step. It often seemed that although I worked through the day and far into the night, and even though I did everything I could, nothing would ever be enough. I remember one night in particular.

I was in my study praying—or trying to pray—and the hopelessness of the situation began to overwhelm me. I felt as though I were suffocating. This may sound exaggerated but it is not. I was curled up in a ball on the floor trying to pray, but I couldn't get my breath. I lay there, hanging on to the leg of the desk, crying out to God in desperation, "Lord, wake Betty up and let her come in here and pray for me. I feel as though I'm dying and I don't want to die." Almost instantly, Betty was kneeling by my side praying. She stayed there for some time until victory came and I was breathing normally and praying with her.

After she went back to bed, I reached up and took my Bible from the desk. I opened it at random, and it fell open at Hebrews 13:20-21:

May the God of peace, who through the blood of the eternal covenant brought back from the dead our Lord Jesus, that great Shepherd of the sheep, equip you with everything good for doing his will, and may he work in [you] what is pleasing to him, through Jesus Christ, to whom be glory for ever and ever. Amen.

I thought, Wow! What a promise—someday I'd like to preach from that text! In other words, I thought the text would make a good sermon, but I didn't apply it to myself. Then I heard the Holy Spirit say within my innermost spirit, "Have you noticed that the author didn't start with himself? He started with God."

Suddenly, I understood. God is the God of the resurrection. The same Holy Spirit who raised Jesus from the dead is the One who has come to live inside of me, to equip me with everything I need. In a flash, I realized that my only hope of survival was to open up my inner being to God's power.

My only answer was to anchor my hope in the fact that I could depend upon God who raised Jesus from the dead— the God of the resurrection. I could trust God to send his Spirit inside of me and make me strong. With this realization came a solid foundation for my faith, and I began to take the first steps out of the valley of depression.

I found an answer to depression that was totally different from the one of which Vickie Pellegrino wrote. I discovered the wellspring was not my own source of strength, my own maneuverability, my own ability to pick myself up, or my capacity to twist and squirm out of my problems. It was such a help to me to learn that God's Word actually speaks to us about the problem of depression. The wellspring I found is the knowledge that the power that raised Jesus from the dead could come within and make me capable of coping with life.

Depression can be traced to at least four causes. Most of us recognize that one cause may be physical. In the story of Elijah, we see that after the Carmel exploit he was physically exhausted, needing rest and food. The challenge had been tremendous; the tension electric. Surrounded as he had been by the guards of King Ahab, Elijah knew that his very life was on the line. Second, Elijah had been on a great emotional and spiritual "high." All day he had watched the prophets of Baal struggle in prayer, even cutting themselves, becoming frantic. Then, after he himself had prayed, fire had fallen out of heaven and consumed his sacrifice. All of that had been a tremendous emotional strain.

There is no "high" like that which comes when we battle through to a tremendous victory. But there is often a letdown after such a high, which seems to be what happened to Elijah. He had experienced a spiritual high, and now he was experiencing a physical and emotional reaction.

Many times my most difficult hours come after having been in the pulpit preaching. During such a time of exhilaration, I forget my worries and those problems waiting in my office. I get caught up in the tremendous emotion of the moment. Then the "amen" is said, and I have to come back down to earth. But then, I'm weary, and the problems I left in the office seem to have grown in size during my absence. It is sometimes hard to remember what I have just said in the pulpit and harder still to act on those words of faith I have uttered just moments before.

There is a close parallel between the physical and the spiritual or between the body and the spirit.

Emotional stress affects the heart, making it beat faster. It causes the blood pressure to rise. Too much emotional stress can cause tension within our physical beings and put our nerves on edge. Other results may be chronic fatigue, even ulcers, and migraine headaches. It is not just poetry to say, "He's a pain in the neck," or "She makes me sick!" Our emotions can cause physical reactions.

Much has been written concerning psychosomatic illness. The implication is that it is "all in the mind." But in psychosomatic disease, the illness is real, and the pain is not just imagined. The mind doesn't actually cause the disease, but the mind and body are so interrelated that they act on each other in an intimate, direct, and inseparable way. Often illness, a very real illness, is the result. On the other hand, when our body is ill—for example, with the flu—it quite dramatically affects our mental state. The one works on the other, irrevocably and continuously.

Sometimes depression is the result of our temperament or personality, or is aggravated by it. For example, we may tend to have more low moods or more high moods than others do. Some people seem to be born with sunshine personalities while others are quieter and given to introspection. Some seem to live a more even existence while others experience extreme highs and lows. In addition to this, none of us lives in an emotional straight line. To do so would mean neither highs nor lows, which would be neither normal nor desirable. Our emotions, our feelings, are as variable as the weather.

Keep in mind that the person who has the ability to soar emotionally as Elijah did, also is capable of going to the depths of despair. For these reasons, even though our feelings are very important, it is a mistake to take ourselves too seriously, and certainly it is an error to judge our spiritual temperature by the way we feel at a given moment.

Of course, there are times when depression comes as a natural result of difficult situations. The truth is, we have problems, and usually there are no fast or easy solutions. I have been depressed and I have had real problems—they were not figments of my imagination. Elijah was not only physically and emotionally exhausted, but he had a very real problem. The queen, who had already killed many of his contemporaries, was determined to kill him.

The Apostle Peter wrote to the Christians who had been scattered throughout Asia because of persecution, saying, "You may have had to suffer grief in all kinds of trials" (1 Pet. 1:6).

Sometimes we may feel depressed because we are harassed by struggles and trouble. We are having a hard time of it, as anyone can see. During such times, if we are not careful, we can get an unreal or one-sided view of the Christian life. We tend to think of the Christian life as an endless experience of trouble and difficulty. There may also be times when we picture the life of following Christ as something that brings only prosperity, joy, and fulfillment.

Peter understood this. In his early days of following Christ he had problems in accepting the fact that death and sorrow must touch his Lord. He and the other disciples wanted the kingdom and they wanted it now! They were concerned with the outward, not the inward.

Later in life, Peter came to realize that the purpose of

God is to make us into the image of Christ, to change the inner person, which can only be accomplished through certain kinds of experiences.

First, Peter said these trials are temporary. Second, they do not come by accident. They are part of God's design. Third, they come to shape us into the kind of persons God wants us to be. Trouble is a part of life. It cannot be avoided, and it comes to all men, great and small. While we acknowledge that trouble is part of life, we also expect Christians to somehow live above their emotions. We tend to see a depressed Christian as a contradiction. I believe we become confused because we fail to understand that:

Conversion is both an instantaneous action and a lifelong experience.

When we accept Jesus Christ as Savior and Lord, his blood cleanses us from all sin and breaks the hold of sin on us. New spiritual life comes to abide within (see 1 John 2:27). However, we do not immediately become like Jesus. We are told to "grow up into . . . Christ" (Eph. 4:15), but such growth is progressive. Becoming a Christian doesn't do away with all our problems. In fact, sometimes it presents us with a new set.

God created Adam a perfect being, but because of the Fall, we the sons and daughters of Adam all enter the world not only spiritually dead but with minds, emotions, and wills suffering the effects of the sinful nature. Adam had a mind that could communicate with the Eternal. That is to say, there was no mental blockage or confusion. God gave man emotions and the ability to express himself freely and openly. There were no negative emotions within man when he was created. God gave man a will; and he lived in harmony with an obedience to his Maker. Then temptation came and appealed to the mind, the emotions, and the will. When man yielded, thereby sinning, his mind, emotions, and will were disturbed.

Picture with me, if you will, three straight wires. Let one represent the mind, the second the emotions, and the third the will, as God created them—straight and whole, without any twists or distortions. Sin twisted those wires. That is, sin caused the emotions to become knotted up, the mind to be warped in its thinking, the will to be bent toward wrongdoing. Finally, sin enclosed man in his problem. It was as if those wires were twisted and bent and then encased in a glass bottle. Such was man's condition before conversion.

At conversion, we were born again, meaning we became spiritually alive, but nothing concerning our minds, emotions, and wills changes immediately. Instead, we grow into maturity. We are born as "spiritual babes" in Christ, but we are meant to grow into mature sons and daughters. As we cooperate with God, we begin to think as God thinks— and the twisted minds become gradually straightened. Furthermore, as we mature, our emotions are healed. As we allow God to work within us, our wills are restored to a straight direction. We grow spiritually from one experience to another.

It is when I trust God and allow him to comfort me in anxious moments that I learn to conquer fear. When I allow him to lead me through moments of frustration, I learn patience. When I yield my will to him and allow him to fill the emptiness of my life with his presence or to redirect my affections or to renew my mind, I experience growth.

And when we can allow God to minister to us in times of depression and learn the biblical steps to take, we can move into joy and hopefulness. I have found four steps that have helped me to cope with depression, and each step is very important. I've learned that I have to take all four because they come in a package.

Step #1: Recognize God is with you in the situation.
If you are deeply depressed, you may not feel God's presence. Like Elijah, you may not be aware of God at all, thinking you are all by yourself. Elijah told God, "The Israelites have rejected your covenant. . . . I am the only one left" (1 Kings 19:10). He even said, "Lord, let me die." Of course, he didn't really want to die. If he had, he could have stayed where he was and Jezebel would have obliged him. He said he did because he was physically and emotionally exhausted.

Probably God will not send an angel to you—at least not in a way you would recognize—but he will make his concern evident. God will make his presence felt because he loves you, and you are of great value to him. He cares about what happens to you. Elijah was valuable to God—not because of his triumph on Mount Carmel—but simply because he was God's child, Elijah.

Most of us do not begin to appreciate our worth to God. Nor do we comprehend the depths of God's love and concern. We are his children, part of a two-way relationship, with the greater weight of love on his side. We love him, but only in a minuscule way when compared with his love for us. He not only loves us, he also understands us (Ps. 103:13-14; Heb. 4:15).

Be assured—God will come to you! The fact is, he is never not with you. He is as surely with you when you are depressed as he is when you are on a mountaintop emotionally. Don't you forget it! "Because God has said, 'Never will I leave you; never will I forsake you'" (Heb. 13:5).

*Step #2: Ask God to help you identify the cause of
your depression.* In an attitude of prayer, honestly asking
God's help, take a penetrating look at your depression. Is it
possible that the cause is physical? Are you, in fact, asking
more of yourself than you are physically able to accomplish?
God has created us not only to work but also to take time
to rest and renew ourselves physically. How long has it
been since you had a complete physical? Are you eating as
you should? What about sleeping? Exercise? Are you taking
good care of your body? Perhaps what is most needed is
rest and an improved diet.

We need to exercise compassion toward ourselves
instead of reproaching ourselves because we become weary
in trying to accomplish impossible tasks. Perhaps a physical
problem is contributing to our mental state of depression.
The Psalmist said that we are "fearfully and wonderfully
made." How true that is! We are only beginning to
understand the inner workings of the mental, physical,
emotional, and spiritual aspects of man. When depression
persists over a long period of time, a medical examination
is in order to determine if there is a physical cause.

It may be that the Lord will help you to see that your
problem is related to your temperament. In this generation
it hardly seems necessary to say, "Learn to know yourself."
In fact, this age, tagged by Thomas Wolfe as the "Me
Generation," seems obsessed with the inner search, with
finding oneself. However, the fact of this obsession does
not do away with the value of learning, under the guidance
of the Holy Spirit, to know yourself, to recognize how you
respond to given situations.

Try to evaluate objectively your situation. It may well be
that you have problems, difficult circumstances, which
naturally make the heart heavy. When some people tell me
about the trials they are going through, I am not at all

surprised to learn they are battling depression.

Step #3: Learn to tap the energy of God. The fact is, we
have an energy crisis. We sometimes find that we lack the
inner resources necessary to face a difficult situation
victoriously. We know that God has all power and that this
power, which raised Jesus from the dead, is at work in us.
But how do we tap this power?

True surrender to the will of God for our lives brings us
into a relationship with God, giving us an open channel to
receive things from God. God is anxious to give to us, but
he will not transgress our wills. As long as we are determined to solve the problem our way, God will not interfere.
When we surrender to his way, we place ourselves in a
position to receive help from him. Through surrender, we
become receptive to his inner suggestions to our spirits.

The Psalmist referred to the righteous man as being "like
a tree planted by the rivers of water," referring to the way
the roots of the tree go down deep to drink from the
waters of the earth. The water is there, but the tree will not
benefit from it unless its roots go down deep. We tap into
God's energy on an hour-by-hour, day-by-day, basis. We
absorb his power as we spend time daily alone with God
in prayer and in meditating on the Word. We feed our
minds on the promises of God, reminding ourselves whom
we are serving and what we believe. By faith we say, "Yes, I
see the circumstances—things are tough. I don't know what
the answer is but God does."

During some of the dark days, an attorney friend said to
me, "Charles, I don't go to your church. I am not a believer
in the same sense that you are, but I have listened to you
preach by television over the years. Now, draw back and
get a hold of the strength that you have always preached
existed." In other words, "Practice what you preach."

Scores of times I have asked myself, "Do I really believe what I have said I believe?" I think most of us know that we only really believe what we put into practice.

I made a choice to believe the Word of God. I began to say, "Yes, I do believe. I will anchor my faith in the Word of God." In those years of testing I found God's Word to be reliable and immutable. I found I could build upon the promises of God and that his Word could be trusted.

Faith works, but it is not automatic. We have to exercise our faith, reminding ourselves of past victories, meditating on the promises of God, keeping our minds open to receiving from God.

Step #4: Take some action. Determine that depression will no longer control your life. Basically, depression is caused by unbelief (our failure to affirm our confidence in God) and self-pity (the feeling that we are somehow being mistreated—and in truth, this may be the case).

Depression is progressive. It begins with a suggestion to our mind or with a feeling that all is not well. It then progresses to brooding. We entertain the suggestion and think upon it, agreeing with it. Finally, depression settles over us like a dark cloud. In so doing, we use our faith to believe an untruth, to nourish our self-pity, and the result is a slide into despair. The longer this goes on, the deeper our discouragement and depression.

Replace negative thoughts with scriptural affirmation. If we are to reverse this situation, we must begin to replace negative thoughts with such thoughts as, "This is the day the Lord has made, let us rejoice and be glad in it" (Ps. 118:24). We need to talk to ourselves as David the psalmist did: "Why are you downcast, O my soul? Why so disturbed within me? Put your hope in God, for I will yet praise him, my Savior and my God" (Ps. 42:11).

Surround yourself with uplifting music and literature. Be careful of the books you read and the television programs you watch.

Read the Word aloud, beginning perhaps with Psalms of praise, such as Psalms 145–150. There is tremendous power in the spoken Word!

Find a prayer partner. Ask God to lead you to someone who can share in prayer with you. One of Elijah's problems was that he left behind all friends and fellowship and went off alone. There is great value in corporate worship and in small group ministries, of people coming together as a group of followers of Christ and sharing their needs and victories with one another. We need each other. Just as the men in space need a support system, we need a network of praying concerned friends to undergird and support us.

Do something for someone else. Last, but not least, reach out to someone in need. You may find that all you can do at first is to give a smile of encouragement or a word of appreciation. The important thing is to take action. Do something today to help someone else. Each time you reach out to someone else who is hurting, you will weaken the hold of depression on your own life, and you will replace depression with joy.

I also discovered that there are four biblical steps out of depression. Before I share them with you, I want to discuss the causes of depression.

STRESS STABILIZERS
Four Steps out of Depression:
Step #1: Recognize God is with you in the situation.
Step #2: Ask God to help you identify the cause.
Step #3: Tap the energy of God.

Step #4: Take some action.

      a. Determine that depression shall not control your life.

      b. Replace despair with scriptural affirmations.

      c. Read the Word aloud.

      d. Find a prayer partner.

      e. Do something for someone else.

NOTES
1. Stanton L. Jones, "Dealing with Depression," *Christianity Today* (September 1982), 60.

CHAPTER FIVE
CAN WE DARE TO TRUST GOD?

I looked into the grieving mother's stricken eyes and ached
for her. I had rushed to the home after learning that the
sixteen-year-old son had committed suicide. She had just
told me, "Pastor, ever since our daughter was taken from us
so tragically nine months ago, I have prayed every morning,
'Lord, put a shield of protection around our children.' . . . I
don't understand. How could God have allowed this to
happen?"

The pain in her eyes took me back many years before, to
other pain-filled eyes. On that occasion I had been called to
St. Joseph's Hospital about one o'clock in the morning in
response to a desperate call from a young man in our
congregation. His wife had just given birth to their first
child. It had appeared to be a routine birth. The young
father nervously paced the floor in the waiting room,
waiting there for the nurse or the doctor to come and
announce the arrival of "a bouncing boy" or "a pretty little
girl." When the doctor broke the sad news that his child
was not normal, he called me and I came immediately to
be with him.

I will never forget the way he grabbed me when I walked in. He clutched the lapels of my coat and pulled me up close. His face was only a couple of inches from mine. He looked deep into my eyes and with a quivering voice said, "Pastor, the doctor says that my boy was born hopelessly crippled." Then with tears streaming down his face he said, "Pastor, I am not ready for something like this."

Just recently I stood beside the grave with four six-foot sons and a grandson, to bury the woman who was their mother and grandmother. Her life had been taken by cancer, and the home-going seemed too soon. The question on the lips of those sons and the grandson was the same, regardless of age. "Why did God take her?"

I could go on almost endlessly, recounting stories like those, which focus on the almost unanswerable questions in life. Unexpected tragedy is the story of life, and the Christian is not immune.

We are seldom, if ever, prepared for deep tragedies that threaten the very foundations of our faith or for the questions they bring. The assault on our faith can be terminal unless we are firmly rooted in truth. We can understand why people respond as they do when they look at the suffering and inequity in life and ask, "How can anyone acknowledge that all this is happening and still believe in a loving God?"

I know what it feels like to walk with God, to trust him, and then to have the unthinkable happen. I think back to days in this decade when darkness seemed to fall upon darkness. Like trip-hammer blows, devastating events came into our lives—the collapse of the financial structure of three organizations of which I was president, each having to file for bankruptcy under Chapter Eleven; having to face investors who needed their money desperately, and having nothing to give them; a fire in our home; the loss of personal assets; divorce in the marriages of our children; the mysterious death of a young man whom we had grown to love; an indictment by the grand jury and a criminal trial; and the loss of friendships within and without the church.

My life was out of control. Inside I was screaming for help, and I could not keep the questions from rising to the surface: "Do I dare to trust God with my life? Is God really in control? If he is in control, why is all this happening to me?"

The questions tumbled out, one after another. The painful events seemed to swirl around me, and I felt I was caught in the quicksand of doubt and despair. I was angry and I was afraid. In the darkness of the night hours, I longed for morning to come and then dreaded what the light of a new day would bring. Tossed about by fear, tormented by doubt, I went again to the Word for an answer. I knew that faith must have a resting place—there has to be a safe anchorage, somewhere on which faith may fasten. To climb up a ladder, one has to have that first rung to step upon.

I began reading in Acts 27. An account is given there of the Apostle Paul who was on a ship crossing the Adriatic Sea. For fourteen days and nights the ship had been tossed about by a storm. Luke explained, "Fearing that we would be dashed against the rocks, they [the sailors] dropped four anchors from the stern and prayed for daylight" (Acts 27:29). Like those sailors of old, when my storm became the wildest and I felt my life was out of control, I too dropped four anchors and prayed for the dawn.

Sooner or later we have to struggle with such questions as: Is God all-powerful? Is God really in control? Does God involve himself in our affairs?

It really comes down to a question of trust. For if the answer to any of those questions is no, then we are faced with a dilemma. "Can we dare to trust God with our lives?" If we cannot trust God in everything, what happens to our faith? If we cannot trust God in every area of life, then the very foundation of our faith is weakened. If we have to put limits on our trust in God, our faith is weakened. Finally, our faith is shattered, and we are overtaken by fear and torn apart by the storms on the rocky shore of life.

I have long ago given up the struggle to find the perfect answer to that very personal dilemma. For nothing less than the total healing of a crippled, deformed son would really satisfy the devastated parents in their hour of deep pain. Unless the tragedy or loss can be undone, the grieving parents will not be totally happy.

The struggle is personal because each of us must face this crucible of life by ourselves. We must test the mettle of our faith in God against those uncontrollable forces and win our individual victories.

So I do not attempt to give answers that satisfy everyone. However, I can share the four anchors that have held me steady in my own hour of fierce storm. These truths have helped me to minister to scores of others who walk those incredible pathways of sorrow and hurt. I have been able to cope with the stresses of life because of my anchors:

Anchor #1. God is all-powerful. Arthur W. Pink, one of my favorite authors, said, "There is infinitely more power lodged in the nature of God than is expressed in all his works." Most of us know something about the power of God's works—the thunder that rocks the heavens, the display of his power in a thousand different ways in the natural world as well as the manifestation of his power in our own lives. Arthur Pink was saying that the very nature of God is strength and power. This is the message of the prophets of old: "Lord, I have heard of your fame; I stand in awe of your deeds" (Hab. 3:2). "You rule over all the kingdoms of the nations. Power and might are in your hand" (2 Chron. 20:6). "These are but the outer fringe of his works. . . . Who then can understand the thunder of his power?" (Job 26:14). "Who has measured the waters in the hollow of his hand, or with the breadth of his hand marked off the heavens? Who has held the dust of the earth in a basket, or weighed the mountains on the scales and the hills in a balance?" (Isa. 40:12).

It is no wonder that the Psalmist David said, "Power belongs to God." It is great to know that there is no one in heaven or on earth or in hell who is greater than God. He is omnipotent. It is into the light of the greatness of his power that we bring our fears, our frustrations, our problems, our needs.

Not only is God omnipotent, he is also omniscient. He is all-knowing. God is aware of everything that happens. "He views the ends of the earth and sees everything under the heavens" (Job 28:24). "He knows the secrets of the heart" (Ps. 44:21). "Who has understood the mind of the Lord, or instructed him as his counselor? Whom did the Lord consult to enlighten him, and who taught him the right way? Who was it that taught him knowledge or showed him the path of understanding?" (Isa. 40:13-14).

Isaiah asks the question, "Where did God get his knowledge? Who taught him?" Did you ever stop to think that in order for God to create the universe as we know it, this masterpiece of terrestrial architecture, that he had to understand all the mathematical disciplines of science? He had to be a super-mathematician. He had to be an ultra-physicist, chemist, philosopher, and astronomer. Man struggles to gain a limited understanding of how the human mind works. God, on the other hand, designed and created the mind.

God is also omnipresent, which means that he is

everywhere present at the same time. There is no place one can go to get away from God. God is everywhere present in his universe. God is not a thought; he is not a memory; he is a presence. " 'Can anyone hide in secret places so that I cannot see him?' declares the Lord. 'Do not I fill heaven and earth?' declares the Lord" (Jer. 23:24).

The Psalmist David wrote,

You discern my going out and my lying down; you are familiar with all my ways. . . . Where can I go from your Spirit? Where can I flee from your presence? . . . If I rise on the wings of the dawn, if I settle on the far side of the sea, even there your hand will guide me . . . even the darkness will not be dark to you; the night will shine like the day, for darkness is as light to you. (Psalm 139:3, 7, 9-10, 12)

God has said, "Never will I leave you; never will I forsake you" (Heb. 13:5). For us, that is good news, isn't it? God sees even in the darkness. To God darkness is the same as light. The eyes of the Lord are everywhere keeping watch, which means that even in our darkest hour, even when we feel there is no light left, God is there and he sees and understands.

God is sovereign. Sovereignty means that God is "boss" in his universe. He created everything. He is all-powerful. He knows all. He is everywhere present and his voice is final. He has the final word. "The Lord is the true God; he is the living God, the eternal King" (Jer. 10:10). "The Most High is sovereign over the kingdoms of men" (Dan. 4:17). "His dominion is an eternal dominion; his kingdom endures from generation to generation" (Dan. 4:34).

God has the last word. Standing in our pulpit one dramatic day was one of the world's great people, the late Corrie ten Boom. She told the story of a tense night in Holland. The city was being bombed by the Germans, with bombs dropping so close that she feared for her life, and she could not sleep. She heard her sister Betsy down in the kitchen, so she went down and had a cup of tea with her.

After awhile the bombs ceased dropping, the night became quiet, so Corrie made her way up the circular stairway to her bedroom. As was her custom, without turning on a light she reached down her hand to smooth out the pillow. As she did she struck something on her pillow. It was a sharp, jagged piece of metal, about ten inches long. It was so sharp that it cut her hand, which started to bleed. She quickly went downstairs and called for Betsy. As Betsy was binding up the wound, Corrie looked up and said, "Betsy, if I hadn't heard you in the kitchen . . ."

"Don't say any more," Betsy said to Corrie, "because there are no ifs with God. Our security, Corrie, is in the fact that we know that God knows everything."

That's what it is all about. Otherwise, it is just so much theology. God knew the shrapnel would hit; he knew Betsy would go to the kitchen, that Corrie wouldn't be able to sleep and would go down to the kitchen at the precise moment that a piece of shrapnel would hit her pillow. Had she not gone, Corrie would have been no more; but God had plans for Corrie. Those plans included a concentration camp, yes, but also a book, and later a film called *The Hiding Place.* His plans included a testimony that brought tens of millions of people into a consciousness that God is a great God. God knows. He understands. The God we serve today is also available.

Anchor #2. God intervenes in the affairs of men. The people in Isaiah's day were complaining, saying God wasn't fair: "Why do you say, O Jacob, and complain, O Israel, 'My way is hidden from the Lord; my cause is disregarded by my God'?" (Isa. 40:27).

In the light of Corrie's story and ten thousand other stories that people could share, how can we doubt? Over and over in the Scriptures God assures us that he does care. David wrote, "As a father has compassion on his children, so the Lord has compassion on those who fear him; for he knows how we are formed, he remembers that we are dust" (Ps. 103:13-14).

Jesus said, "Are not two sparrows sold for a penny? Yet not one of them will fall to the ground apart from the will of your Father. And even the very hairs of your head are all numbered" (Matt. 10:29-30).

Jeremiah wrote, "His compassions never fail. . . . Great is your faithfulness" (Lam. 3:22-23).

The Apostle John wrote, "This is love: not that we loved God, but that he loved us and sent his Son as an atoning sacrifice for our sins" (1 John 4:10). And in another place, "How great is the love the Father has lavished on us, that we should be called children of God! And that is what we are!" (1 John 3:1).

God cares, and he communicates this caring to his children. When I am aware that the nature of God is to talk to his children, it means a great deal to me. When we begin to get an idea of how great God is and of his creative genius, we can be overwhelmed. We can get the feeling that while God cares, there is a great space between him and us. But when we link this awareness with the knowledge that he talks to individuals, that he knows our names, that he communicates, it changes everything. Again, time after time, God in the Scriptures reminds us of that fact. "Moses spoke and the voice of God answered him" (Exod. 19:19). "He will call upon me, and I will answer him" (Ps. 91:15). "Call to me and I will answer you and tell you great and unsearchable things you do not know" (Jer. 33:3).

The Bible emphasizes the fact that God becomes involved in our affairs. David spoke of God's intervening in his life: "He parted the heavens and came down. . . . He reached down from on high and took hold of me; he drew me out of deep waters. He rescued me" (2 Sam. 22:10, 17-18).

Who was it that came down? God. He parted the waters. He took hold of David. He brought him out of deep waters. He rescued him. The personal pronoun emphasizes the all-powerful God, the all-wise God.

Moses wrote, "What other nation is so great as to have their gods near them the way the Lord our God is near us whenever we pray to him?" (Deut. 4:7). The prophet Hanani reminded King Asa, "For the eyes of the Lord range throughout the earth to strengthen those whose hearts are fully committed to him" (2 Chron. 16:9).

The Lord spoke through Isaiah, "For I am the Lord, your God, who takes hold of your right hand and says to you, 'Do not fear; I will help you' " (Isa. 41:13). In another place he said, "When you pass through the waters, I will be with you; and when you pass through the rivers, they will not sweep over you. When you walk through the fire, you will not be burned" (43:2).

These are the promises from the Word of God. These promises are immutable, absolutely positive. They can be depended upon in all kinds of stress and strain.

We rejoice in these scriptural promises, but they do not quite completely answer the questions that arise in times of tragedy, incurable illness, sudden business reverses, or untimely death. The third truth that holds me steady in the storm of doubt is:

Anchor #3. God is in control. We need to consider three things in this regard. First, God's will toward us is a good will (John 10:10). When God created us he did not have in mind for any one of us to fail. God created us and endowed us with the ability to be creators and to succeed.

Second, when God created us in his own image, he created us with an awareness of our need of himself. Never did God plan for any man to be independent of his Creator, nor to be self-sufficient within himself.

No man, without living in right relationship with God, can ever be a whole person.

One of man's unique distinctions is his capacity to know God. Man is created to enjoy fellowship with God and to live in relationship with him. Man can know God as surely as he can know his neighbor.

Third, man was given the freedom of choice. God has limited his own intervention in the affairs of men because he will not invade or override man's will.

God, by his Spirit, comes to us and invites us voluntarily to surrender our will to him. We have the ability to accept his invitation and surrender our will to him or to reject him. Until we do surrender our will to him and come to know God, we are not whole persons. Apart from God, man is incomplete. Many people refuse to surrender their will to the will of God. They simply say, "I don't need God. Whatever life deals out to me, I can handle. I'm able to erase my own erroneous zones. I can forgive myself, therefore, I don't need God."

Or some say, "I don't believe there is a God, so I am going to eat, drink, and be merry because tomorrow I may die and that is all there is—there is no hereafter."

On the other hand, the man who recognizes that he is in need of God, that he has failed, feels guilty and in need of forgiveness, and understands that God loves him, will find salvation through the Lord Jesus Christ. The grace of God is released to the one who asks for the full pardon of God and surrenders his will to him. Spiritual life is imparted to him, and he becomes a child of God. He is born into the family of God and comes into an understanding of his kinship to God. He understands that in Jesus Christ he becomes a whole person, complete—not yet mature, but complete. If he serves Jesus for fifty years, he will never be more complete in Christ than he was the first moment he became a Christian.

God will not override man's free will, for to do so would be to negate that "free" will. God could have created men as robots, without the possibility of sinning, but man would have been limited in his own being as well as being limited in his relationship with the Father. So God chose to grant mankind the gift of free will, and in so doing he put limitations on his own intervention.

Man, in choosing to disobey God, opened himself to the entire aftermath of that sin in the form of disease and decay.

At the beginning of this chapter I mentioned a young man in our congregation who took his life. I said on the occasion of his funeral that I really did not believe that God allowed this to happen to teach any of us a lesson. I knew that lessons would be learned, and they should be. We should learn all we can because of what has happened. In fact, we should never be the same again. But I do not believe that God permits these things in order that he might stamp indelibly on us a lesson that he wants us to learn. In tragic situations like those, people are prone to ask, "Was God in control? If he is in control, why didn't he stop this from happening? Either God doesn't care or he is powerless to prevent things like this!"

Yes, God is in control, but he has given us freedom of choice. He has given us the gift of free will even knowing what we might do with that gift. God wants us to be persons and not puppets. He gives us the opportunity, the privilege, and the responsibility of making decisions. God gives control to us for the direction our lives will take. As persons we must make decisions because that is part of the essence of life.

In moments of tragedy, such as when someone we dearly love makes a wrong choice, we face the temptation of making God our adversary instead of our advocate. We face a temptation to make God an enemy right at the very time when we need him most as a friend. Instead of turning toward God for the comfort we need and he wants to give, we turn away and our sorrow is deepened.

Anchor #4. We can dare to trust God with our lives. Jesus Christ gave us a portrait of God as a loving heavenly Father. At the time when Jesus walked and ministered on the shores of Lake Galilee, the world was filled with sickness and suffering. It was a world of wickedness and hate, a world experiencing earthquakes and famines. Mental illness was rampant. People were often killed by crucifixion. One historian spoke of that time as a period of extra-ordinary degeneration. History books record that in Rome alone lived 1,300,000 slaves owned by 2,000 lords. Often, these owners were very cruel to their slaves.

Yet, in the midst of that world, Jesus said, "Take heart! I have overcome the world!" (John 16:33) and "Do not worry about tomorrow, for tomorrow will worry about itself" (Matt. 6:34).

I believe one tremendous truth undergirded the life of Jesus. It was a theme that ran through every chapter of his life. It is a truth that is expressed by John in these words: "The Lord God omnipotent reigneth" (Rev. 19:6, KJV).

Jesus knew that God his Father reigned. The confidence behind his thinking, the power behind his every heartbeat, the very breath he breathed, rested on this truth.

If you and I could bring every problem, every sphere of life, into the light of this truth, we would begin to see how powerful it is. The fact that God exists and that he reigns in full power means he is all-powerful—he is omnipotent. He is the sum total of all the power of the universe, and he reigns. He is my God, and because he reigns, I can bring my worry or my fear to him and I can find a release. I can be confident that he will take care of every need I surrender into his hands.

For God to be free to intervene, I must release my problem into his hands.

God is in control of all I place in his hands. But, you may respond, "Look around you at the sin and turmoil in the world. Tell me, is God really in control of this?" The Book of Revelation, from which the above verse was taken, has a background of blood, smoke, and martyrdom. In its chapters the Rome of the Caesars and the church of the Galilean are locked in mortal combat.

The first Nero endeavored to smash the hopes and the dreams of the saints. In Revelation the kings of the earth take counsel against Jesus Christ and the eternal God. A word portrait is given of the second Babylon, drunk with the blood of Jesus' friends. You can see people intoxicated by the unholy task of the sin, debauchery, and remorse. By the time the reader comes to the end of chapter 18 of Revelation, he would expect the writer to say, "Man, the battle is lost. The cause of Christ is ruined." But not so! In chapters 19–22, we read that the battle is won with a resplendent and eternal victory. The writer of Revelation said, "The Lord God omnipotent reigneth." Why? Because back of the Caesars, back of the blood, back of the smoke, back of all the sin that is rampant, there reigns an eternal God, One whose throne is above the earth. He will triumph!

The Psalmist expressed a similar theme to that of the writer of Revelation. The Psalmist looked across the ages, seeing the horror of the engulfing waters rising higher and the destruction and the sorrow. Seeing the sorrow, the heartache, and the suffering, he wrote: "The Lord sits enthroned over the flood; the Lord is enthroned as King forever" (Ps. 29:10).

The Psalmist was saying the same thing as John in Revelation. When the floods of life come, when the rains descend, and sorrow beats against our lives, when our dreams are at our feet in a thousand pieces, when we are at the breaking point, remember, "The Lord sits enthroned over the flood." The Lord God Omnipotent reigneth—even in those shattered dreams, in our broken plans, in our sorrows. In those dreadful moments we can look to that text and know that God sits on the top of the flood, that he is King forever. We can know that God is not overwhelmed, and that he is working in the situation for our good (Rom. 8:28).

I do not begin to know all the answers to life's great mysteries. But this I do know: God reigns above my worry, my inadequacy, the sin that I am wrestling with, or the sorrow that has engulfed my life. The Lord God Omnipotent reigneth! With that comes a quiet peace, an inner knowledge that indeed I can dare to trust God.

I love these words of St. Francis de Sales:

Be at peace.
The same everlasting Father
who cares for you today
Will take care of you

tomorrow and every day . . .
Either he will shield you
from suffering
Or he will give you unfailing strength
to bear it.
Be at peace then, and put aside
All anxious thoughts and imaginations.

Will these anchors hold? The fact that this book is being written is testimony to the holding power of these truths. I have been tested beyond what I thought I could bear, but never beyond his sustaining grace. I have been crushed by loss and pain, but not overwhelmed by those events. Time and again, the storm clouds have threatened this flimsy craft, but the anchors held me fast.

I shall ever be grateful that I did not have to face the storm alone, that my dear wife, Betty, stood faithfully by my side, praying for me and encouraging me.

STRESS STABILIZERS
1. God is all powerful!
2. God intervenes in the lives of men.
3. God is in control.
4. God reigns over the flood. We can dare to trust God with our lives.

CHAPTER SIX
ONE BY ONE, THE PROPS WERE KNOCKED AWAY

The auctioneer stood by the beautiful leopard, mounted with its paws lying over a log, as though it were alive. When the auctioneer cried, "Sold," I tried to choke back the tears, but one slid down my cheek just as the television news camera caught me full face.

Over the years big game hunting had been a hobby— one I was able to pursue as an extra benefit of going overseas on missions trips. Sometimes when I would preach at mission stations I would also arrange a safari, to bring back a trophy and some pictures to show the men. In all, I had accumulated some forty-five trophies. A friend of mine is a taxidermist, and he would finish my trophies gradually during his off-season. I soon had too many trophies for our home to accommodate. One was a polar bear that stood on his hind legs (eight feet tall). I finally put it in the Fellowship Hall at the church because there was no other place large enough. My favorite was the beautiful leopard I had taken in Kenya.

Behind each trophy was a story, and each was important to me. So, when the Lord showed me that I should sell those trophies and use the money to pay back the debt, it was tough on me.

However, when you owe money, and you are in a valley, you begin to evaluate what really is valuable to you. As I did, the trophies became less valuable.

To run the auction, we arranged with one of Colorado's best auctioneers, a Christian and a good friend of ours. Many from the congregation gave sacrificially of their "treasures" as well, so there were many other things along with my trophies to be auctioned. I watched as, one by one, my prized trophies were sold and carried away. The bear sold for $5,000; the leopard for $4,000. That day we raised $50,000, which was applied toward our debt.

In the process of that experience, I had to examine my attachment to possessions. Our Lord spoke out about materialism or the mercenary spirit, which he knew could get a hold of any of us. He waged war against it because he knew:

Attachment to possessions complicates life. The love of money causes untold emotional stress.

The Arabic word for wealth is *mammon*. This word is still found in some translations of the Bible. Jesus said very clearly, "No one can serve two masters. Either he will hate the one and love the other, or he will be devoted to the one and despise the other. You cannot serve both God and Money [Mammon]" (Matt. 6:24).

Jesus looked at wealth as a rival god. He said one cannot give his allegiance to wealth and at the same time put God first in his life. Later Jesus warned, "Be on your guard against all kinds of greed; a man's life does not consist in the abundance of his possessions" (Luke 12:15).

I have gone through some real moments of frustration in

regard to possessions. I can laugh about them now as I look back, but it wasn't funny then. I remember standing in my study at the church one night, talking on the phone, when I heard a fire engine race by. I said, "It sounds like a real fire—I wonder if my house is on fire" (we lived a couple of houses down the street). *Ridiculous*, I thought, then a second truck drove by. When the fire trucks did not return, I decided to check.

Betty, who was there in my office with me, turned to me and said, "You're joking, but I am afraid it may be true! I'm leaving now!" I followed her. We went out the back door of the church, across the parking lot, and down the street. As we got closer I realized that the fire trucks were in our driveway. The ladders were up at the back window. The firemen had chopped out the upstairs windows, and the smoke was rolling out. We stood there watching, not knowing whether the whole place was going to go up in flames or not.

The home was owned by the church. It was a beautiful English-type mansion, which looked like an old castle. It was so large that it had seven bathrooms. We had agreed to move in there just nine months before, after selling our home. The place had been devastated by water—many of the pipes had frozen, then broken and flooded during the previous winter when no one was living there. Before the fire occurred, we spent nine long months getting the whole thing back into shape. I should say, rather, that Betty spent nine months because she either did the work or supervised having it done.

That very day of the fire, Betty had placed the last flower arrangement on the table in the center of the living room. The redecorating was complete.

We left for church with the satisfied feeling that at last it was finished. Now, we stood and watched the smoke roll out of the windows. Finally—hours later—2:00 A.M. to be exact—one of the firemen told us that the fire was out, but that we could not stay in the house. He advised us to go in and get our valuables.

We lost a lot of things that night that were very precious to us. We had assumed that the church had household insurance for the contents, and the church thought we did. We discovered that the house itself was insured, but nothing else. When we learned what was gone—many things were irreplaceable that we had gathered from around the world—and that we wouldn't get any money to replace them. It caused frustration, to say the least. This happened right in the midst of our financial problems, so there were no resources to replace our losses.

We got the house cleaned up and repaired after three long months of working with several different contractors. Most of the damage was in one room. The rest was smoke damage. We had scarcely moved in again when it was determined that the church had to sell the house. That year, problem piled upon problem, and at times we wondered if there would ever be an end to it all. We rented a small house and lived there for almost five years until the Lord provided different housing.

That was not the last loss we would face. Another severe test came for us during the final payoff of the church's indebtedness. Following five years of quarterly payments, the church had to make one final, large balloon payment that represented the interest due the creditors on their investments. As we approached the deadline, we decided to try to break this large amount down into amounts due individuals so it would be easier for the congregation to visualize the task. We took each of the claims and put that exact amount on a paper "brick," which we attached to the side walls of the sanctuary, which were also brick. Then we asked the people to believe and pray with us and give as God directed them. We challenged them to "take a brick," to give an offering to make possible the repayment of one or more of these individual claims. There were no names, only claim numbers on the back of the paper bricks with the amount due on the face. Slowly the bricks came down as monies were given. In addition, some investors donated their investments. As each brick came down, the total amount due was reduced.

One of those claims belonged to Betty and myself. It was a $29,000 obligation, which represented the equity from the sale of our home that we had invested in the ministry. As I said, at that time we were living in a rented house. This "brick" was all we had left of a lifetime of savings. Everything else had gone to pay legal fees. As I was praying, I felt the Lord say to me, "Charles, I want you and Betty to donate your $29,000 investment."

Well, I wrestled with that! It was not easy. My future was unknown. I thought of Betty and the children. It took some time, but I wrestled through it and, at last, I was willing to obey the Lord. Then I blew it. It was Saturday evening. I went home, walked by Betty, who was working in the kitchen and said, "Betty, God said for us to give our $29,000 certificate."

Instead of being tender and kind, instead of realizing that she would have the same struggle I had, instead of being understanding and offering to pray with her about it, I just told her. I have apologized to her since for my lack of consideration and sensitivity. I simply said to her in passing, "The Lord told me to do this, and we'll do this tomorrow."

Naturally, my announcement left her in a tailspin. People had warned her that I would probably die of a heart attack before the financial struggle was over. If that happened, the

$29,000 was all she would have. Without that, she felt she had no security whatsoever. I think her struggle, in consequence, was far greater than mine had been. The next morning, I stood in the pulpit and said, "The Lord supplied another need. Some people are giving a $29,000 investment." Nobody knew it was ours, not even our children. I said, "As you know, we have had different ones take the bricks down and bring them up here as the money has been given. Today, I would like Betty to go get the $29,000 brick."

I thought that would help. I'm ashamed to say that I was oblivious to the real depth of her struggle. I sensed she was reluctant, but I did not begin to understand. If I had, I would have known that asking her to bring me the "brick" was not helpful. Later, she shared this story with one of our television audiences. I'm including it here because she can tell her own story better than I can.

When Charles walked by me on Saturday night and said, "Is it okay if we give our $29,000 tomorrow?" it startled me so I couldn't get an answer out. It took me awhile. Finally, I said, "I guess so." I knew the moment I said it that I did not have a willing heart. I was having a real struggle. In fact, I didn't dare tell him what a great struggle it was. My mind was surging, rolling, and tumbling with questions. "God, that's all I've got when I get old. What am I going to do? That's all the security I have."

I also knew that it was twenty-five years of house payments. I remembered the times of really struggling to make those payments. That claim represented security to me in old age. I wrestled with it until finally I said, "God, I am ashamed of myself—I've got to go to the bedroom and pray." So I did. I thought, I can't go to Sunday school in the morning and teach my class if I have this attitude, with this spirit, in me. It is terrible. *I awakened in the night and prayed again.*

Sunday morning found me in my usual spot, seated at the organ. In the middle of the service, I heard these words from my husband, standing in the pulpit: "Folks, someone has given us this gift today of $29,000 toward the debt, so we want to take the brick down. Betty, would you like to go get the brick and bring it to me?"

I thought, Oh, God, he is really doing it! I had hoped that he might change his mind. I thought, I can't believe it. He really is doing it!

I slid off the organ bench. I felt the tears coming up and about to spill over. All I could think of was, Smile. Everybody is looking at you. Smile! *I thought,* I can't smile. I'm about to cry. *I could have walked across the front to the other side to take the brick down, but I slipped out the side door to go around by the back hallway and in the door on the other side. I knew that I was buying time by taking the long way around. In so doing, I passed by the back door. I had a great urge to walk out and keep on walking. But I didn't. I walked around and came in on the other side. I finally got the "brick" and took it to Charles.*

We stood there together and he said, "Betty, would you like to pray?" *Well, that was it. At that point the dam burst and I said,* "I can't." *I cried, and he prayed. After the prayer I went back to the organ.*

The next day the struggle was still going on within me. Several ladies were coming by for lunch. They sensed the difficulty of my struggle and suggested we pray together. After the prayer time, the Lord brought to my attention a most beautiful Scripture. When I read it, I couldn't believe the words I was hearing. I have it marked in my Bible—August 13, 1980. It is Mark 10:28-30: "Peter said to him, 'We have left everything to follow you!' 'I tell you the truth,'

Jesus replied, 'no one who has left home or brothers or sisters or mother or father or children or fields for me and the gospel will fail to receive a hundred times as much in this present age (homes, brothers, sisters, mothers, children and fields—and with them, persecutions) and in the age to come, eternal life.' " When I really saw the truth of that verse, such a joy flooded my heart that actually I haven't had a moment's thought from that day to this of what will happen when I am old. I almost get a bit giddy when I think—Jesus is going to take care of me when I get old!

This struggle for Betty and me was not to be the end of our testing. In 1981 a book was released written by John and Elizabeth Sherrill and me, entitled *The Man Who Could Do No Wrong.* That book told of the events of our greatest difficulty.

The story took two years to write. The title of the book was taken from an article that appeared in *The Denver Post,* which was called: "The Man Who Could Do No Wrong." As the book went to press, I got a call from John Sherrill. He said, "Charles, as you travel from city to city autographing books, you are going to be interviewed by the press. The press is going to tear you apart if you take royalties on that book." He named others who had had similar experiences, Chuck Colson being one. "You will be accused of writing the book in order to use the difficulties you have experienced these past years to make money." Then John said to me, "Why don't you pray and ask the Lord what he would have you do about the royalties?"

I said, "I don't need to pray. I am going to use that money to pay some of my debts."

He said, "Fine. If that is what the Lord has told you. But I just want you to know, the press is going to crucify you and accuse you of writing the book for that purpose."

Well, to give up the royalties was like selling my trophies and giving our Calvary Temple investment. That was the last straw. This time I did remember to talk it over with Betty, and I recall how we became weak-kneed and began to tremble and say, "Another prop is pulled out from under us. What are we going to do?"

Obviously, if you have read the book you noticed on the back page it says: "Charles Blair has donated all royalties from the sale of this book to Calvary Temple and its ministries." I say that just to emphasize how interesting it is that God takes us through these experiences to teach us to be dependent upon him. I think perhaps I struggled over giving up the royalties as Betty did with the $29,000 "brick." Finally, I too had to let go and trust myself into God's loving hands.

Betty and I have both learned from these experiences that when our confidence is fully in God, we experience a release from anxiety.

If the very heart of our being is a life of faith, a core of trust, then we have a release from anxiety.

I love the words of Dietrich Bonhoeffer on the subject of anxiety and possessions. He said:

Earthly possessions dazzle our eyes and delude us into thinking that they can provide security and freedom from anxiety. Yet all the time they are the very source of all anxiety. If our hearts are set on them, our reward is an anxiety whose burden is intolerable. Anxiety creates its own treasures and they in turn beget further care. When we seek for security in possessions we are trying to drive out care with care, and the net result is the precise opposite of our anticipations. The fetters which bind us to our possessions

*prove to be cares themselves. The way to misuse our
possessions is to use them as an insurance against the
morrow. Anxiety is always directed to the morrow, whereas
goods are in the strictest sense meant to be used only for
today.*[1]

This is not to say that a Christian should not have
material wealth. I am emphasizing that:

Our security must not rest in our possessions.

The Word of God teaches us that true financial security
comes when we are free of a mercenary spirit, when we
are no longer worried because at the center of our lives is
trust in God. He gives all that we have to us, and he is able
to protect what he gives. If he takes away, he can give
back.

When Betty and I lost everything we had, we reread the
Book of Job. We knelt down, held hands, and prayed
together: "The Lord has given. The Lord has taken away.
Blessed be the name of the Lord!" We believe that when
God gets through testing us, he is going to give us back all
that we have lost.

We lost our house; he has given us another house. The
Lord miraculously provided a down payment. I can now
drive a nail in the wall and put a picture on it and it is my
wall. I am paying it out in payments, but it is mine. God is
restoring to us what we have lost.

The Psalmist declared, "I shall not want" (Ps. 23:1). Betty
and I have learned that we can dare to trust God to take
care of our financial needs. God was calling Betty and me
to a more simple life-style. Combined with trust in God, we
found the core of financial security.

Finding the life-style that is right for you, one that pleases
God and leads to security, is an individual matter.

A number of years ago, Betty and I agreed on a certain life-style that we felt was right for us and pleasing to the Lord. Then we determined the amount of salary needed to provide that life-style. We agreed that any additional income above that amount would be given to the Lord. This practice has been a very freeing experience for us. As the Lord dealt with us in matters of finances and life-style, we grappled with five questions. The first of them was:

1. *Why do you purchase certain things?* For example, a car. Do you buy a car for utility or for prestige? A house for its livability or to impress somebody? Clothes? Do you need the items, or are you just keeping up with fashion? Did you know that we sometimes crave things that we neither need nor enjoy? Now, isn't that strange? We buy things that we don't want, in order to impress people whom we don't like. We are ashamed to wear clothes and drive cars that are out of step with fashion. We judge people by what they produce, how much they are worth, or how much they earn, instead of by who and what they are.

Our society is sick because it is fractured, fragmented. It doesn't have a unity around which life flows. If we conform to our sick society, it is an indication that we are sick ourselves. The believer is to have a divine center, and that is the presence of God. Around that center will flow all that he is, all that he does, and all that he has. The writer of Ecclesiastes said, "Whoever loves money never has money enough; whoever loves wealth is never satisfied with his income. This too is meaningless" (5:10).

Isaiah wrote, "Why spend money for what is not bread, and your labor on what does not satisfy? Listen, listen to me, and eat what is good, and your soul will delight in the richest of fare" (55:2).

The Bible does not teach that money in itself is evil or that having money makes life complicated. Betty Rollin, author of *First, You Cry,* said of money, "Happiness, as everyone knows, has nothing to do with money. Except everyone is wrong. Money alone won't do it, but money is one of life's great garnishes. There's nothing like having it on the side."[2]

And most of us have learned that not having money hurts. Not having money means not being able to provide adequately for our loved ones. Not having money can be very limiting. So it is not money, but a mercenary spirit that is the problem. A mercenary spirit always asks, "What is there in this for me? What do I get out of this?" It is the *love* of money that is the root of evil, says the Scripture, the mercenary spirit that grips people and causes them to lose touch with reality. So, the important question to ask ourselves is, what is our motivation in wanting this possession?

2. *How many things have a hold on you?* Coffee? Alcohol? Coca-Cola? Tobacco? Television? Movies? Chocolate? Simplicity is freedom. We ought to refuse to be a slave to anything, except to Jesus.

Many of the pressures that we have today in our world are the result of our pursuit of possessions. We have been duped into believing that luxuries are necessities. We have become anxious and troubled about nonessentials, convincing ourselves that the things we want are what we must have.

Jesus said in very plain language, "Be on your guard against all kinds of greed; a man's life does not consist in the abundance of his possessions." Matthew recorded his words: "What good will it be for a man if he gains the whole world, yet forfeits his soul?" (16:26).

My wife was inspired by the verse, "God has said, 'Never will I leave you; never will I forsake you.' So we say with confidence, 'The Lord is my helper; I will not be afraid.

What can man do to me?' " (Heb. 13:5-6). I thought that
was a great verse, and I committed it to memory. I leaned
upon it, but later I noticed the first part of that fifth verse,
which hadn't attracted my attention before: "Keep your
lives free from the love of money and be content with what
you have, because God has said, 'Never will I leave you;
never will I forsake you.' "

It is this desire for the accumulation of things that leads
to our being trapped into the pursuit of possessions.
Someone has said that a hundred years ago the average
person had 72 wants. Of those 72 wants, there were only
17 that were necessary for the carrying on of daily life. A
hundred years later, the average person has 484 wants and
94 of these are considered necessities. One hundred years
ago there were 200 items which people were urged to
possess. Today, 32,000 (and more!) articles are advertised.
We are bombarded on every side with the message that the
acquisition of things will bring us happiness.

3. *How freely do you give things away?* Two kinds of people
live in this world—the takers and the givers. Which
are you? Do you accumulate or do you dispose? What do
you do with what you have? Do you sort it, store it, dust it,
then sort it again, store it, and readjust it? That is
complication!

4. *How easily are you sold?* On a recent flight, I picked up a
little pamphlet which read, "Fly now. Pay later." It is so easy
to be sucked into easy payments that turn out to be very
difficult. They can trap a person into bondage. We don't
have to have the finest of everything. If we insist on trying
we complicate our lives.

All of us can determine whether a thing is worthwhile.
The simple rule is this: "If a thing is really worthwhile from
God's point of view, you always have to pay the price first
and enjoy its benefits later. If it isn't worthwhile, you can

enjoy its benefits now and pay the price later."

5. *What are you doing today that keeps you from doing the real thing?* What are you doing today that keeps you from being the person you have always wanted to be, and from doing the things you always wanted to do, and that God wants you to do?

Anne Brown, in one of her books, told about three businessmen, all brothers, in the southern part of the United States. They had a comfortable business. Because of their expertise in a certain field, they were given the opportunity to gain a controlling interest in a new invention. Their part would be to manufacture and market the invention. In return, they could become rich.

They analyzed the product and came to the conclusion that an unlimited opportunity was theirs. They also determined that in order to develop and market this invention, they would have to work day and night and focus all their energies in that direction. After considering these factors, they declined the opportunity. Their reasons for declining were significant. They said, "We are family men and we are Christians. We have a good business and are making ample profits. When the day's work is over, we can spend the evening with our families. We have energy to give as officials in our church. We are excited about what Christ is doing in the world, and we want to have time for the church and for him. Therefore, we will not take any situation that is presented to us if we have to lose our values to gain money we do not need."

Jesus was not telling us to sell everything we own and go out with a begging bowl. He was saying, "In your striving to get to a higher level of living, be very careful that you don't lose something that is even of greater value."

He reminded us that satisfying the craving for things is an endless task, a hopeless venture. If we try to do something because the Joneses are doing it, we must be careful. About the time we catch up with the Jones family down the street or around the corner, we will discover there is another Jones family, and they have a little bit more. Somebody asked John Rockefeller how much money it took to satisfy, and he said, "Just a little bit more." Our pressure may be brought about by our own doing because of our pursuit of possessions. In the striving for possessions we may find ourselves with many things to live *with* but very little to live *for*. In so doing, we can miss some of the great values of life.

Sometimes we need to stop and listen to an inner voice and ask ourselves if the strain we are under, the pressures we are enduring, are the result of unworthy ambitions. Not only do we get caught up with a materialistic philosophy of just wanting to accumulate things, we are also caught up in trading true greatness for worldly acclaim.

Christ was not saying that it is wrong to have influence. It is not wrong for one to want to be in a position of rank in order that Christ may be glorified. He was saying, "Be careful lest in the striving, lest in the accumulation of things, you lose that which is of greater value—the spiritual dimension that comes only by taking some time at my feet."

I read with a great deal of interest a research paper by Dr. Richard Gordon, a psychiatrist on the East Coast. He made a survey of young suburban couples in a large city. He said:

The only word I can use in describing the young junior executive, the young couple caught up into this whirl of social obligations and appointments is tension. They follow a dizzy whirl of meetings and parties until they are so physically exhausted they turn to stimulants. This group of people is determined to get to the top at all costs. The one word that I can use to describe their condition physically is simply tension, tension, tension.

In an interview concerning the survey, he was asked what a person should do about this problem. He said, "I think when people find themselves getting tense and under great pressure that they ought to stop and ask themselves, 'Is this worth the trouble?' "

The answer to this striving for possessions and goals— and it is a very beautiful answer because it comes from the sacred Scriptures—is to surrender our ambitions, our plans, and our dreams to God. I say this from experience. I have discovered that if I have a goal that is God's goal, his goal becomes my goal. This means I am moving in God's direction. When I move in his direction, I have his blessing. When I have his blessing, his power operates in my life, for wherever his blessing is, his power is there also.

When I go at God's pace, I have peace. Inward peace is the opposite of pressure. It is tranquility; it is a joy unspeakable, an indescribable peace. It gives a dimension to life that doesn't rob me of ambition or initiative or the excitement of living. It simply means that I am doing what God wants me to do and I do it for the glory of God.

It is the center in our life that makes the difference. If we have God in that center, there is trust. When our trust is in God, and we choose to live simply, we can be at peace.

STRESS STABILIZERS
Two secrets of release from the anxiety of possessions: Simplicity is an inward spirit of trust in God. The more simply you live, the more security you will have.

Five questions that help us to simplify our lives:
1. Why do you purchase certain things?

2. How many things have a hold on you?
3. How freely do you give things away?
4. How easily are you sold?
5. What are you doing today to prevent you from doing the real things?

NOTES
1. Dietrich Bonhoeffer, "Giving Tomorrow to God" *Christianity Today* (16 September 1983), 54.
2. Betty Rollin, "What's So Bad About Being Happy" *First, You Cry* (New York: New York Times Co., 1982).

CHAPTER SEVEN
STEPS TO COPING WITH FEAR

It was 4:00 A.M. and I was awake, pacing the floor. For several nights I had had trouble sleeping. I would toss and turn, and when I finally dropped off to sleep I would wake early. I struggled with fear because it seemed that I faced an impossible task.

Following my conviction in August of 1976, I was placed on probation for five years with the stipulation that I remain in Denver and use my influence in raising funds to repay the investors of Calvary Temple, Life Center, and The Charles E. Blair Foundation. Each of the three entities was struggling through Chapter Eleven proceedings and was committed to making quarterly payments to its creditors. Calvary Temple was on a five-year repayment plan, with scheduled large quarterly payments. Each quarter it was a struggle right up to the last moment to make those payments. In addition to participating in making the church's quarterly payments, many of the members also gave sacrificially to help make Life Center and the Foundation's quarterly payments. Not one payment came easily.

I remember clearly one particular Calvary Temple payment, which was due September 19, 1977. Four weeks before it was due we had $2,000 in the bank toward the required amount.

The devil began to torment me and say, "I've got you now! You're not going to be able to make this payment, and I'll tell the world that you are in default." As I walked the floor that early morning, I began to visualize the newspaper headlines and I felt my stomach knotting up. I reminded myself of the faithfulness of the people in giving, but the challenge of raising thousands of dollars in four weeks' time above regular expenses—there at the end of the summer—seemed overwhelming.

Something about the wee hours of the morning makes the coming tasks of tomorrow seem almost impossible to perform. In the aloneness and darkness of that hour, we have a tendency to lose our nerve. We try to force ourselves to go to sleep in a hurry, and it is impossible. We get that "three o'clock in the morning feeling" because we know that in just a short time the dawn comes and the battle begins. When dawn finally comes, we are drained from loss of sleep and worry.

That morning, I knew I had a problem and it was not money. I sensed that fear was taking hold of me and canceling out my faith. I knew I dared not succumb to this tormenting fear, so again I arranged to take a few days and go to the mountains to a condo, which a friend had made available to me. I knew I needed to get quiet before God and let him speak to me.

There, in my friend's condo, I sat on the floor in the bedroom and began to read the Bible, starting with John 14 and 15. I read aloud the promises that Jesus gave, that if I would ask the Father for anything in his name, he would give it. I turned to Luke 6:38 and read where Jesus said,

"Give and it shall be given unto you." I reminded God that Betty and I had been giving faithfully—it was part of our lives—and we were now due to begin receiving. There, in the stillness of that room, surrounded by the majestic mountains, hearing myself read aloud the great promises of the Word, I began to remind God of his promises. I turned to Mark 11:24 and read, "Whatever you ask for in prayer, believe that you have received it, and it will be yours." I determined that the Word of God would be my guarantee; the very blood of Jesus Christ himself guaranteed those promises.

I decided, come what may, I would base my faith on the eternal Word of God.

I then began once again to search for a man in the Scriptures who faced a similar situation, and my attention was drawn to King Asa in the Old Testament. Asa was king of Judah and commander-in-chief of the army. On this occasion he and his men were surrounded by an enemy army that outnumbered them in men and equipment.

In the blackness of the night, as the men awaited the dawn and were poised to react to any sound in the night, Asa was in his tent praying. Asa was a godly king who had destroyed the altars to foreign gods, had commanded Judah to seek God, and had rebuilt the walled cities. For some time, the country had known peace and prosperity, but now Zerah the Cushite and his vast army had marched against Asa.

Asa knew there was no earthly way for his army to slip by the Cushites; they were trapped with no chance of a truce. Only one thing was left to do—face the enemy and fight their way out. Yet they were vastly outnumbered. So all night the king wrestled in prayer.

He reminded God of his greatness, which is a wonderful habit. Like David of old who, when he faced Goliath, recalled how God had delivered him from the lion and the bear, so Asa remembered past victories and built up his faith. He said, "Lord, there is no one like you to help the powerless against the mighty." He reminded God and himself of God's ability to bare his arm and come to the rescue of his children (2 Chron. 14).

As I read that passage, I too began to recall the numerous times God had intervened. I recalled that each step thus far had been a struggle, but that as I had put my trust in God and followed his leading closely, step by step, God had sustained me.

I was learning in a new way what it meant to stay close to God and listen for the direction of the Holy Spirit in each circumstance. During that time, Rex Humbard came to see me. He is a good friend, and I love him dearly. He came to preach on a Wednesday night. He paid the way for three attorneys and brought them with him, men he thought might help us. We spent several hours together, discussing the problem.

After the attorneys had gone to their hotel, Rex went home with Betty and me, and we spent still more time talking. It was then that he said to me, "Charles, I have been talking with ————," and he named three other outstanding evangelists and spiritual leaders, "and we have decided to rent Mile High Stadium and have a telethon to help you get through this financial crisis. We are going to fill that stadium with men and women and have a telethon unlike any America has ever seen. These men and I are doing this because we love you and want to help."

I got really excited to think that those men would willingly come to Denver and help bail us out. It felt good to feel their love, and their offer gave me new hope. That night I prayed about it, and I heard God say softly in my spirit, "No, not the Big Five but the Big One. Just Me. I don't want you to hold the telethon."

I could scarcely believe it, but I knew God had spoken to me. So I called Rex and said, "You're not going to believe this, but I prayed about your offer and God said, 'No.' "

There was silence on the other end of the line for a time and then Rex said, "He did?"

I reaffirmed what I felt God's direction had been and then added, "I don't know what God wants, but I hope he has a better idea. For right now, I don't feel the telethon is the right thing to do."

I believe God expects his children to stay tuned to that "still small voice," to know when he is speaking, and to listen and act accordingly. I was reminded again that, as with Asa, my dependence must be on God. My task was to follow closely in obedience.

After a night of wrestling in prayer, Asa had a breakthrough. A peace came into his heart, and with a calm and steady voice he declared, "Help us, O Lord our God, for we rely on you, and in your name we have come against this vast army" (2 Chron. 14:11). (The last three words in the King James Version are "against this multitude.") I circled those three little words. I knew that my situation was different, but yet it was similar. I, too, faced a multitude of problems. I felt surrounded and overwhelmed. I didn't see any way out.

Life has a way of hemming us in by a multitude of anxieties and complications—the scramble of business, the strain of competition, the burden and the heat, the wear and the tear, the fuss and the hassle, the thousand and one fears—paralyze our faith. We are confronted with the insecurity of feeling young and inexperienced, or the loneliness of growing old. Most of us have learned that life is real, and it is a battle. We face a real enemy. We are not just shadowboxing.

Second, I focused on the words, "O God, we rely on you." Most of us cannot say that. If we are honest with ourselves we have to admit that the restfulness to which Asa refers, the poise within his spirit, the tranquility of his inner being, are things we seek but seldom experience.

The biblical record shows that, with God's help, Asa and his men were victors: "The Lord struck down the Cushites before Asa and his Judah. . . . They were crushed before the Lord and his forces" (2 Chron. 14:12-13). Even as I read and prayed and rejoiced in the faithfulness of God, I felt God directing me to still another passage: "Cast all your anxiety on him because he cares for you" (1 Pet. 5:7).

It was as though God were saying to me, "You don't have to carry the load alone. Give your problem and your fear to me. Let me fight for you."

Believe me, it didn't take me long to take God up on that offer. I gathered up all the fear, rolled all the weight of that quarterly payment into a neat package, and symbolically handed it to God. I felt a thousand pounds lighter. I knew I had anchored in the promises of God.

I got up, walked out into the living room of the condo, and said to Betty, who had accompanied me, "If the money were in the bank for this payment, what would my actions be?"

She said, "You tell me."

I replied, "I would just be praising the Lord that the money was in the bank for the payment. I would go down there to Denver and preach the gospel and use my energy to meet the needs of the people. And that's the way I've got to act because faith is the substance of things hoped for; it is the evidence of things not seen."

That's exactly what I did. The first one to hear me say so

was the devil, and he kept on saying, "It isn't going to
work. It's not working!"

Each time Satan taunted me, I would reply, "Shut up. It is
working!" and he would say, "You need a lot of money.
This faith talk is just so much talk—you're going to end up
with egg on your face!" So it went—I was harassed by the
enemy for weeks. But he lost.

The more fear Satan tried to dump on me, the more I
countered with the promises of God. Fear and torment left
because the love of God is released when we act upon the
promises of God and love drives out fear.

In that experience I discovered four steps to coping with
fear. They are: (1) Face your fear, (2) Review your
resources, (3) Replace your fears with praise, and (4) Give
your fear to God.

1. *Face your fear.* Fear operates best in the shadows
where we cannot see its weaknesses. It abides in
semidarkness or in the twilight zone. Shadows have a way
of making harmless objects appear bigger than life. A
squirrel on the roof, a mouse in the closet, or any noise in
the night becomes more threatening than it is in daylight.
Fear is not as powerful as it would have you think, nor are
you as weak as you may feel in the midst of life's
turbulences.

Several years ago, I took a trip around the Aleutian
Islands on the way into Seward Harbor in Alaska. I was
among twelve passengers on a dirty cargo ship, which was
traveling very slowly. We ran into a storm, and I
thought the old wooden ship would crack and fall apart
from the stress. We were standing on the deck, holding on
for dear life. I was up on deck because I was seasick—so
sick I thought I would die, and then afraid that I wouldn't. I
asked an officer that day, "Do you think the ship can stand
the pressure of this storm?"

I have never forgotten his reply. He said, "This boat is built to ride out the worst of storms."

The same could be said for you and me. We are built for the best and the worst that life can give us, providing we allow our faith to go deep in God. We lose sight of that truth when we allow our fears to hide in the shadows. Fear, if allowed to control us, blows the situation out of proportion. When we bring our fear into the light, we can put it into perspective. We must ask ourselves, "Is this fear realistic, considering the problem I face, or has my imagination gone wild?" Fear is inner panic. It gives us the sense of having lost control. When we look fear in the face, we regain control and have taken the first step to coping with it.

We may discover that the thing we fear is really fearful. The important thing is that by bringing it out into the light we can look at it directly, see it clearly, and begin to work out a plan for coping with it. We are no longer shadowboxing. We are dealing with reality. We know its true size. When we have done this, we are ready to move on to the second step.

2. *Review your resources.* The Apostle Paul reminded Timothy, "For God did not give us a spirit of timidity, but a spirit of power, of love and of self-discipline" (2 Tim. 1:7). God does not will that we be sheltered from the storms of life. He does promise to go with us through the storms and to give us peace.

Catherine Booth, wife of General Booth, founder of the Salvation Army, was reluctant to accompany her husband on his adventure of faith in taking the gospel to the down-and-outers in London, England. In her distress, she went to prayer. Later she reported, "When I saw Jesus, he did not smile at me. He did not chide me. He just raised his hand, and in that hand I saw the nail print. Then I heard him say to me, 'There is no other way. This is your way.' "

To which Catherine replied, "Lord, so be it. Will you go with me?"

The Lord's answer to her was, "I will be with you to the very end."

In their years of ministry, Catherine and General Booth went to the ends of the earth. Though they paid a great price, they held on to the promise of "the presence of a living Savior." This was the truth Paul talked about in one of the most difficult times of his life. He said, "But the Lord stood at my side and gave me strength" (2 Tim. 4:17).

One day a telephone call came from a young preacher friend of mine who was dying. He said, "Charles, there is no hope for me in the natural world. I am going to die. I wonder if it would be possible for you to come and spend some time alone with me. I want to be sure that I am right with God. I have some things that I need to share in confidence. I have asked myself whom I should call to come, and I thought of you. Will you come?"

Naturally, I laid aside everything, got on an airplane, and flew to his side. Medical science had done all it could, and he had been allowed to go home so that he could die amid familiar surroundings. After I shared greetings and talked awhile with family members, he dismissed them and the nurse so we could be alone.

When his lips became silent following the confession, prayer, and praise, I sat silently, holding his hand. It seemed like an eternity; no words were spoken, there seemed to be nothing more to say.

Then I felt a squeeze of my hand and he very softly said to me, "Charles, Jesus just spoke to me."

I didn't reply for a few minutes, but finally I broke the silence, and, calling him by name, asked, "Can you share with me what Jesus said?"

He looked at me and said, "Charles, he just said, 'I've been with you, and I'll go with you through death.' "

When the young preacher did go home to be with the Lord, which happened soon after our conversation, the family reported a radiance in the room unlike anything they had ever experienced.

Fear blinds us and causes us to forget that we do not face our problems alone; we have resources. First and foremost, God is the source of our supply. The Scriptures are packed with affirmations that God is the source of prosperity and desires to give to his children.

"May those who delight in my vindication shout for joy and gladness; may they always say, 'The Lord be exalted, who delights in the well-being of his servant' " (Ps. 35:27).

"Wealth and honor come from you" (1 Chron. 29:12).

"When his master saw that the Lord was with him and that the Lord gave him success in everything he did, Joseph found favor in his eyes" (Gen. 39:3-4).

"But remember the Lord your God, for it is he who gives you the ability to produce wealth, and so confirms his covenant, which he swore to your forefathers, as it is today" (Deut. 8:18).

"I am the Lord your God, who teaches you what is best for you, who directs you in the way you should go" (Isa. 48:17).

"But seek first his kingdom and his righteousness, and all these things will be given to you as well" (Matt. 6:33).

"And my God will meet all your needs according to his glorious riches in Christ Jesus" (Phil. 4:19).

"Every good and perfect gift is from above, coming down from the Father of the heavenly lights, who does not change like shifting shadows" (James 1:17).

God is the source of our supply—a simple yet profound statement. It is in him that we find the answer for our problems. It is God's adequacy which is always greater than our need.

Fear also paralyzes our creativity and causes us to overlook possible solutions that are at our fingertips. Fear nullifies our abilities and makes us feel we are smaller than the task that confronts us. Focusing our attention on God as the source of our supply rather than on the problem releases us to find solutions.

3. *Replace your fears with praise.* It doesn't work to get up one day and say, "I'm not going to be afraid any more." Or, "beginning at 12:30 A.M., I'm not going to worry any more." None of us can live in a vacuum. We have to put something in place of the fear that we reject. I recommend replacing fear with praise, because that is what the Scripture teaches us:

Rejoice in the Lord always. I will say it again: Rejoice! Let your gentleness be evident to all. The Lord is near. Do not be anxious about anything, but in everything, by prayer and petition, with thanksgiving, present your requests to God. And the peace of God, which transcends all understanding, will guard your hearts and your minds in Christ Jesus. Finally, brothers, whatever is true, whatever is noble, whatever is right, whatever is pure, whatever is lovely, whatever is admirable—if anything is excellent or praiseworthy—think about such things. (Phil. 4:4-8)

When we choose to reject the fear and focus on praising God, our reward is the peace of God, which sets up a guard around our minds and inner spirits, bringing tranquility.

I have learned to do that by basing my praise on a promise of God. That is, I commit to memory a nugget of truth and apply it to my situation. For example, in Joshua, the promise is given, "Do not let this Book of the Law depart from your mouth; meditate on it day and night, so that you may be careful to do everything written in it. Then you will be prosperous and successful" (1:8).

Knowing that God has made this promise helps me to have confidence that God is going to be my helper. I know that God is greater than anything mere man may try to do to me. Therefore, I no longer have reason to be afraid. To affirm that, in the face of fear, is God-honoring, and it is the shortest way to inner peace.

4. *Give your fear to God.* When you give something to someone, you transfer ownership. I remember trying to illustrate this while I was preaching in a citywide crusade in Hong Kong in 1970. I took an American ten-dollar bill out of my pocket and said, "If one of you will come up here, I will give you this ten-dollar bill. It is my gift, with no strings attached."

I waited as the interpreter told the audience what I said and there was no response. I thought they had misunderstood what I said; but finally a little boy got up and made his way to the platform. He zipped across the platform and stretched out his hand. I gave him the ten dollars, and the crowd responded by clapping their hands.

When I gave the boy the money I transmitted ownership—it was no longer mine. This is what the Word of God teaches us to do with our fears. Peter wrote, "Cast all your anxiety on him because he cares for you" (1 Pet. 5:7).

Betty and I were having dinner in a restaurant one evening several years ago when I looked across the room and saw Mr. J. C. Penney, the now-deceased founder of the well-known J. C. Penney stores company. I recognized him by his white hair. I said to Betty, "Do you think it would be rude if I interrupted him and introduced myself?"

I stood by his table for a moment until he looked up, and I said, "Would you accept my apology for intruding, but I would just like the pleasure of shaking your hand."

He said, "Please."

Then he introduced me to his wife and I said, "Mr. Penney, I was just a young man when I was hired by your New York office to work in the J. C. Penney store in Enid, Oklahoma. On one occasion you came to speak to the employees and told us that you had learned to give God ten cents out of every dollar. It made an incredible impression on me. You gave credit to God as your senior partner for becoming very wealthy and having this chain of stores.

"It was during that time that God called me into the ministry. I went to Mr. Ely, the manager of Store 191 in Enid, and he was so pleased with my decision that he helped to support me in Bible college."

Mr. Penney said, "I know Mr. Ely very well. He has gone on to his reward now, but his two sons are in the ministry." Then he asked me, "Have you read my book, *The Ninth Decade?*"

When I replied that I had not, he asked for my business card and said, "I will mail you an autographed copy."

In that book, Mr. Penney told about having had a nervous breakdown when he was but a young man in his early twenties. He had one small department store at the time in a little town in Wyoming, not far from Denver. It was during the depression, and the business had become too much for him, causing his breakdown. As he was recovering in the hospital, one Sunday afternoon he heard through the open door of his room some Christian young people singing, "God Will Take Care of You."

From his hospital bed, Mr. Penney said something like this to God, "Is that just a song, or is it true?" Then he heard an inner whisper, "It is true. If you will turn your problems over to me, I will take care of you."

J. C. Penney said, "God, I'll make a deal with you right now. I'll take you as my senior partner, and I'll turn the business over to you and run it for your glory. We will be partners, and I'll turn over to you the burdens and problems that I am unable to carry if you will heal me and give me strength."

Mr. Penney told in his book of how healing began on that day, as God gave him strength. He went on to become very successful, with some 1,600 stores across America. The turn-around came when he turned his cares and his fears over to God.

His story reminds me of another true story. Standing in our pulpit a few years ago was a man of God by the name of E. Stanley Jones. I remember as if it were yesterday the story he told:

I went to India as a missionary, but came home broken in health. As I was praying one day, stretched out, recovering from a nervous breakdown, I said, "Lord, I don't know what to do with my life. I want to be a missionary but I am broken. I couldn't stand the cultural shock and I went to pieces." God spoke to me and said, "Stanley, are you ready to do what I called you to do?" "No, God," Stanley replied, "I am not ready." God replied, "Stanley, if you will turn it over to me, I'll send you back to do what I called you to do, and I'll give you the strength to do it." That day I made a bargain with God. I said, "God, that's a good deal. I'll go, and you take care of me."

E. Stanley Jones did go, and he wrote *The Christ of the Indian Road*, which became a best-seller, and sixty other books. He preached in India for forty years and was still preaching at the age of eighty-four. At eighty-five, he went to be with the Lord. His life turned around, from an emotional breakdown to a life of victory. The change came when he gave his fears to God.

Corrie ten Boom, author of *The Hiding Place,* came to our church, Calvary Temple, to preach. She brought her purse, which was twice as big as most. She used that purse to illustrate how some people come to the altar to pray. She would take one item at a time out of the purse and lay it on the pulpit as she said, "Lord, this is one of my fears which I lay here on this 'altar.' It has to do with my finances. I've carried this fear long enough, and I can't carry it any longer; so I am giving it to you."

Then she reached in and got another item, which she used to represent another burden. She continued to do this until the purse was quite empty. Then she said, "This is what God wants us to do. He wants us to lay our burdens on the altar, to give our fears and cares into his safekeeping. We lay our burdens on the altar, then when we get through praying, we gather them up and walk out the door." As she said this, she took each item one at a time, which she had laid on the altar, and placed each back in her purse, went over, and sat down.

I have never forgotten the impact of that illustration. How true it is with so many of us! We lay our burdens at his feet and then pick them up and take them with us. When we give our fears to God, he wants us to transmit ownership—to leave those fears with him. The Psalmist said, "Commit your way to the Lord; trust in him." Jesus said, "Come to me, all you who are weary and burdened, and I will give you rest. Take my yoke upon you and learn from me, for I am gentle and humble in heart, and you will find rest for your souls."

Although these four steps are not a cure-all nor an instant

solution, as you put them to work in your life, you will experience a growing ability to cope with fear.

STRESS STABILIZERS
We are built for the best and the worst that life can give us, providing we allow our faith to go deep in God.

Four steps to coping with fear:

1. Face your fear
2. Review your resources
3. Replace your fears with praise
4. Give your fear to God

CHAPTER EIGHT
HOW TO COPE WHEN GOD'S CHASTENING COMES

When the verdict "guilty" was read at my trial, I felt my life, as I had known it, was shattered. Ten years later, on the anniversary of that occasion, my wife, Betty, and I shared with the Calvary Temple congregation our reflections on that decade. It took the form of a dialogue. What follows is a condensation of that talk we gave that day.

Charles: The past ten years have been very difficult. On more than one occasion, we have felt the eyes of the city upon us. Yes, even the eyes of a nation. Today, Betty and I are still here—not because we are special, not because we are tough. We are here because of God's sustaining grace. On reaching this milestone we want to share with you a little of what God has taught us in these years of difficulty. I remember well a phone call that Betty received from Bob Pierce, the founder and president of World Vision. Until his demise, Bob was a close friend of ours and, in fact, his last sermon was preached in this [Calvary Temple] pulpit. In that late night phone call, he said to Betty, "It will take ten years at least before you are able to evaluate this crisis."

There was a great deal of truth in Bob's words, although I didn't want to hear it at the time. It is easier now to look back and evaluate what God has been doing in and through our lives. Betty, can you put in a nutshell your evaluation of the crisis?

Betty: Undoubtedly, this past decade has been an advanced course in God's love. He loves us so much! He sees what lies ahead in the way of pitfalls, of pride, of self-indulgence, of other dangers in the world. He wants to guard us from them, so very often the ways he works in our circumstances cause us to be rerouted onto his course.

I know I am a different person today because of these experiences. I have a note in the margin of my Bible that says, "The greatest thing God does *for* us is what he does *in* us."

Charles: C. S. Lewis wrote, "God whispers to us in our pleasures, speaks to us in our conscience, but shouts in our pain; it is his megaphone to arouse a deaf world."[1] As Betty and I reviewed past events, we asked ourselves, "What one thing does a person need in order to go through ten years of trial or through any other difficult experience? What is the biblical principle?"

We came up with one word, *endurance*. The New American Standard Bible translates Hebrews 10:36, "For you have need of endurance."

Betty: To endure means "to continue in the same state without perishing"; "to remain firm under suffering"; "to bear up." It also means "a state or capability, of lasting in pain, or going through hardship without being overcome."

Charles: I suppose every one of us, in the midst of trial or some overwhelming problem, would like to be able to endure the situation without falling apart. As we discussed this topic, Betty and I determined three reasons why we believe every Christian needs endurance. The first reason is that we are in a spiritual warfare. Life—spiritual life—is a fight. There are no victories without struggle. The Apostle Paul wrote to the young man Timothy and said, "Fight the good fight of the faith" (1 Tim. 6:12).

Life is a fight—it really is—and I don't think it is going to get easier. I think that as the coming of Christ draws closer, we may experience more spiritual warfare; oppression by the enemy will increase.

In his second letter to Timothy, Paul advised him to "endure hardship with us like a good soldier of Christ Jesus" (2 Tim. 2:3).

Betty: Suffering usually goes with warfare. Soldiers don't expect a life of ease and all the comforts of home when they go into the service of their country. They know they are on a mission and have a duty as soldiers. Any one of us may be endangered by a life of ease. We know that, down deep, but we don't like the idea of giving up the ease. The media portray a life of ease, a life of luxury, as the ultimate goal. Actually, in God's economy, life is designed to have problems. Difficulties in our lives "make" us. As I have studied the Scriptures, I have discovered that the great heroes were men and women who had problems. In the midst of their problems they learned to seek God and to let God work through them in furnishing the courage, the strength, the power, and the grace to stand true. As a result, they became instruments who glorified God.

Charles: Another reason we need endurance is so we won't become weary in doing good. We all know that doing wrong can become wearisome, that being disobedient can produce exhaustion. It is also true that we can go on and keep our vows to God—bring the Lord his tithe, keep our prayer life up, abstain from evil and even the appearance of evil, live a holy, separated, sanctified life—and also become weary. There is clearly a weariness that can come from "doing good." We may not have said it aloud but we may have thought, *I'm tired of going to church. I'm tired of reading my Bible and praying. I'm weary of all this.* Weariness sets in, because we are in a spiritual warfare. The heaviness of the times is settling down, which requires us to have endurance. The Scripture says, "We will reap a harvest if we do not give up" (Gal. 6:9). So if we plan to reap, we dare not give up. Paul gave almost the same exhortation to the Thessalonians: "As for you, brothers, never tire of doing what is right" (2 Thess. 3:13). Christians become weary, their spirits droop, they become exhausted, mentally and physically, with the problems of life. And the enemy taunts them by saying, "All this is happening because you are a Christian."

To summarize then, the three reasons why we need endurance are: (1) We are in a spiritual warfare. Life is a struggle. (2) We are living in days when our faith in Christ is being tested. (3) We can be overcome by weariness. Few of us question the need of endurance, but the big question is, How may we acquire it? Betty and I think we have found the scriptural answer. To discipline us, God can use any set of circumstances that comes, whether through our own actions, or through his sovereignty, or through adverse happenings of life. Sometimes the discipline comes through a divorce or through financial reverses. Sometimes it comes through desertion, bereavement, disease, or illness. In all those experiences, we can realize that God is guiding us, sometimes even chastening us. Sometimes unique circumstances encircle our lives. Things happen that we never dreamed would happen. How we respond to what happens can determine the degree to which we understand the discipline of the Lord.

Betty: The writer of Hebrews talks about the Lord's discipline and how not to react to it:
"My son, do not make light of the Lord's discipline, and do not lose heart when he rebukes you, because the Lord disciplines those he loves, and he punishes everyone he accepts as a son." Endure hardship as discipline; God is treating you as sons. For what son is not disciplined by his father? If you are not disciplined (and everyone undergoes discipline), then you are illegitimate children and not true sons. Moreover, we have all had human fathers who disciplined us and we respected them for it. How much more should we submit to the Father of our spirits and live! Our fathers disciplined us for a little while as they thought best; but God disciplines us for our good, that we may share in his holiness. No discipline seems pleasant at the time, but painful. Later on, however, it produces a harvest of righteousness and peace for those who have been trained by it. (Heb. 12:5-11)

Charles: If I am God's child, I will be disciplined. It is God's way of taking the events of life and through them developing and maturing us. I dare not treat discipline lightly, nor refuse to pay attention. I am obligated to respond, "God, you allowed this. What are you trying to teach me through it?"

Betty: The Psalmist wrote, "Before I was afflicted I went astray, but now I obey your word. You are good, and what you do is good; teach me your decrees" (119:67-68).

I remember a preacher saying, "I like life better my way." But we are sons and daughters of God, and we know that God has a greater purpose and reason for our lives than just ease and enjoyment.

Charles: Danger number two is that we dare not faint. During these troubled years, I have often turned to the experiences of David for help and comfort, especially when I have found myself asking, "Why me, God?"

One incident from the life of David stands out in my mind. David had been anointed by Samuel as the new king, but Saul remained in power, not recognizing David as God's choice for the throne. Instead, Saul used his energy to try to destroy David. On this occasion, David had fled with his family and a contingent of faithful men to the land of the Philistines and was living in the city of Ziklag. At first, the Philistines welcomed David and used him and his men more or less as a guerrilla detachment. However, the Philistines later became suspicious and decided to disarm them. When David and his men returned from meeting with the Philistines, they found that the Amalekites had attacked and destroyed their temporary homes and had taken captive their wives and children. As if that was not enough to deal with, David's men—pushed now to the edge of their endurance—turned on him, cursed him to his face, and debated as to whether or not they should stone him.

In that moment of great despair, one might have expected that David would ask, "Why me, God?" Instead, we read these words, "But David found strength in the Lord his God" (1 Sam. 30:6). David did not deal with his problems by denial or by stoical resolution. Nor did he question God and ask, "Why me?" Instead, he turned to the Lord his God. I can almost hear him saying, "Saul has tried to kill me. The Amalekites have robbed me. My own men have all but stoned me. But one thing they cannot do is to prevent God from coming down into this situation and rescuing me!" David could take courage because he knew that God still reigned, that God was in control. That kind of faith could help him declare, "I shall not die but I shall live and declare the works of the Lord." There comes a time in our lives when, as an act of faith, we have to place ourselves in the hands of God and trust that he is in control, that he is working out his plan in our lives.

Betty: I remember well a dream I had in November of 1974, in the early years of our crisis, prior to Charles' grand jury indictment. I believe God gave me the dream to help me endure what would happen.

In the dream, I was walking with my husband in what appeared to be a giant underground parking lot, under a shopping mall. It was unpaved, the floor being uneven, of freshly excavated dirt. It was apparent that new buildings were being built. Charles was in front, leading what seemed to be a large crowd. I couldn't see the people, but I sensed that they were there behind us. It was as though he were directing a tour. He was talking to the crowd as he was leading them. It seemed to go on indefinitely. I couldn't see the end.

He was saying, "This is what I built, and this is what I have built, and this is what I have built." And the thought came to me, *Oh, I don't see any end of this, God. Where does it end?* I looked on ahead and as far as I could see, there was no ending.

Then, an overwhelming impression came to me. "God, this is going to cave in. I'm afraid this is going to fall on us. We have to get out of here," I said. I ran ahead, looking for a ramp, an escape route, and I found a ramp going up.

I started up, and as I got halfway to the exit, a huge trash hauler backed in and began dumping refuse—trash, huge boulders, cinder bricks, and chunks of concrete. All of this came tumbling toward me. My thought was, "Oh, this is a sewer and we are going to be submerged in all of this junk. We shall be killed."

I turned and ran the other way, still looking for a way out. And suddenly I thought, *Where is Charles? Where is he?* I looked over my shoulder and saw him lying flat on his face on the ground, almost completely covered with the refuse. I couldn't tell if he was dead or alive, for only his head was visible. I ran toward him thinking, *I've got to get him out of here.* I wanted to grab his arm and drag him, but the Lord spoke to me clearly and said, "Don't drag him, *lift him up."*

I replied, "God, I can't! I've never lifted 170 pounds in my life."

Then the Lord seemed to say to me, "What do you think you've been in training for all of these years?"

And I answered, "OK, Lord, I can do it."

Somehow, I got Charles on my shoulders and across my back. Frightened, I struggled as I carried him outside and began looking for a place to lay him down. I was thinking, *Oh, if I could only make it to that structure in the distance,* which resembled a bus-boarding shelter I had seen in Europe.

I finally made it to the shelter and as I bent over to lay' Charles down, I caught a glimpse of his face. I was startled because it didn't look like him. Instead, he had the face of a young man. When I awoke, I was sitting straight up in bed. The dream was so vivid. I said, "God, I understand every part of the dream—except the ending."

Then the thought came to me, "He has been 'transformed'!"

This dream and its assurance that God would work

through all that came to us gave me strength in the weeks and years to come. At that moment, I could not comprehend it all, but I knew God had spoken. The dream assured me that God was working, that he would give me strength in the following weeks and years. Many times later I would remember his words to me, "Lift him up" and then, "I will never leave you, nor forsake you so that you may boldly say, The Lord is my helper; I will not fear what man can do unto me."

Those were my bulwarks in the storm. One of the secrets I have learned through all of this is that God has a purpose. James wrote, "Consider it pure joy, my brothers, whenever you face trials of many kinds, because you know that the testing of your faith develops perseverance" (1:2).

Charles: When Betty first told me her dream, I didn't appreciate it. But in time I came to see it as a picture of what God had been doing in our lives. God does take the irretrievable and use it to mold our character. It is true. I am a different person today than I was a decade ago. But it hasn't been easy.

In the midst of such trying circumstances, we may feel as though our very lives are being crushed, as though all the refuse of the world is being heaped upon us. If you have had that experience, as we have, you know how careful one must be lest a root of bitterness should spring up and destroy.

Betty: Submission to the will of God is essential. The title of Dietrich Bonhoeffer's book, *Don't Waste Your Sorrows,* shows great discernment. In the midst of deep problems, I have often found myself reminded of it, and have prayed, "God, don't let me waste this experience. Let me learn what it is that you are teaching me."

During this past decade, there have been times when I

have come close to fainting. If I had dreamed ten years ago that this crisis would have lasted so long, I think I would not have survived. I remember that day in the courtroom at Charles's sentencing, when the judge said, "Can you pay back the $12 million?" and he answered, "I think I can."

I thought, *Oh no, God, that is worse than prison. How can we survive that pressure?* I thought of the congregation, and often I said to Charles, "The most precious thing you have is the spirit of the people. If that is dampened or killed—if you lose that—you've lost it all, you'll have nothing."

Charles: We have learned to live one day at a time. Learning these three things to avoid when experiencing God's chastening have been most important lessons.

We have also learned two positive lessons while enduring chastening, lessons that are equally important. One is to remember that we are *sons,* not *infants.* That is, when we are children, we always think the treatment of punishment is too harsh. It goes a part of being a child. We think, *Dad's too severe,* or *Mom is unfair.* We think, *I don't deserve to be treated this way.* It is easy to stay a child in a crisis and to act as though we were a child and not a grown son or daughter. I believe God would have us respond as grown sons and daughters.

The second point to remember is that our lives are in his hands. God permits what comes into our lives. Nothing can come to us that has not first come through him. He can stop any trial. He is sovereign. He is almighty. He permits these things to occur. We need to remember that our lives are in his hands.

In all that has happened this past decade, God has been with us. We have never missed a meal or a day of work because of illness. God's grace has been sufficient. We have wants, but we have had no needs that have not been supplied. God has sustained us. We have, with James, "seen what the Lord finally brought about. The Lord is full of compassion and mercy" (James 5:11).

FINAL FLASHBACK

Who has not heard of Homer's famous *Odyssey,* his epic travelogue of a ten-year eventful journey? In final retrospect, it now seems to me that our own experiences during the ten years reviewed in these pages might well be called our ten-year *Denver Odyssey.* And what is the biggest thing of all that seems to emerge with shining preeminence? It is this: that the God who permits is the God who directs; that he can transform deepest trouble into truest triumph; that he can teach us far more through adversity than through material prosperity. How many of the great saints have testified to that! How truly, now, Betty and I can endorse their testimony for the encouragement of present-day Christian believers! Listen again to William Cowper, who all through his life was troubled with recurrent illness and other testings:

Ye fearful saints, fresh courage take,
The clouds ye so much dread
Are big with mercy, and shall break
In blessings on your head.

Let us learn to sing afresh with the confident Psalmist. 'God is our refuge [in crisis] and strength [for each testing], an ever-present help in trouble. *Therefore we will not fear"* (Ps. 46:1-2).

STRESS STABILIZERS

The greatest thing God does *for* us is what he does *in* us.
(Betty Blair)

Endurance is necessary for victory because:

1. We are in a spiritual battle (Eph. 6:12).
2. There is the danger of turning away from God.
3. We can be overcome by weariness.

NOTES
1. C. S. Lewis, *The Problem of Pain* (New York: Macmillan, 1948), 81.

BIBLIOGRAPHY

Arnold, Magda B., ed. *The Nature of Emotions.* New York: Penguin Books, 1968.

Bonhoeffer, Dietrich. "Giving Tomorrow to God." *Christianity Today,* 16 September 1983.

Cousins, Norman. *The Healing Heart.* New York: Avon Books, 1984.

Jones, Stanton L. "Dealing with Depression." *Christianity Today,* 17 September 1982.

Lewis, C. S. *The Problem of Pain.* New York: Macmillan, 1948.

Rollin, Betty. *First, You Cry.* New York: New York Times Co., 1982.